MW01504024

The Doorway to Knowing

A Guide to Soulful Living

Cynthia Santee

authorHOUSE®

AuthorHouse™
1663 Liberty Drive
Bloomington, IN 47403
www.authorhouse.com
Phone: 1-800-839-8640

© 2010 Cynthia Santee. All rights reserved.

No part of this book may be reproduced, stored in a retrieval system, or transmitted by any means without the written permission of the author.

First published by AuthorHouse   11/17/2010

ISBN: 978-1-4520-7672-0 (sc)
ISBN: 978-1-4520-7674-4 (e)

Library of Congress Control Number: 2010914234

Printed in the United States of America

This book is printed on acid-free paper.

Because of the dynamic nature of the Internet, any Web addresses or links contained in this book may have changed since publication and may no longer be valid. The views expressed in this work are solely those of the author and do not necessarily reflect the views of the publisher, and the publisher hereby disclaims any responsibility for them.

To contact the author, Cynthia Santee, please visit www.soulself.info

Editing by Heather Babiar, www.ExperiencedEditor.com

This book is dedicated to my sister,
Deborah Lynn Powell –
One of my life's greatest teachers.
(1954 – 2008)
You are loved and greatly missed.

Table of Contents

Preface

I had a powerful experience one cold, January night. This experience began to slowly change my life. It taught me to no longer allow my mind and emotions to dictate my experience; and, thereafter, I consciously decided to become the "captain of my own ship," so to speak. I decided the time had come to allow another aspect of my Self to become my driving force, and to live in a more Self-guided way. I began to understand that the way we perceive our life experiences, and the way we live our lives, is pure choice—it really is as simple as that. However, to allow the consciousness of choice, you have to be open and willing to allow your individualized unfoldment of knowing. As we make a conscious decision to allow our greater awareness to come forth, we choose differently—and, thus, our lives begin to unfold in a whole new way.

My story begins when I try to contact my sister, who lives alone in an apartment and has multiple health issues. On a Wednesday evening, I telephoned her, but there was no answer. I left a message, considering that maybe she was at her friend's apartment, watching TV. I called the next day, on Thursday afternoon, and again, she did not pick up. I surmised that she might have had a doctor's appointment or gone shopping.

Late on Friday evening, I had an unrelenting impulse to call my sister again. I stopped what I was doing and telephoned her, and, again, she wasn't there. Since this was the third day I could not get a hold of her, I became very concerned. I called Terry, one of my sister's neighbors, who indicated that she had not seen her, but said that she would go over to her apartment to check on her. If my sister did not come to the door, she had a key to let herself in. When Terry arrived at my sister's apartment, she found her lying on the floor, unconscious. She called the paramedics. Terry told me that the paramedics had stabilized my sister and that they were taking her to the nearest hospital. She also said that my sister was still unresponsive.

This all occurred around 10 o'clock at night. When I was told of my sister's condition, I immediately proceeded to the emergency room to meet the ambulance. As I drove to the hospital in a state of anxiety, for a moment, I had an odd experience of becoming an observer of my own thoughts, emotions, and energy. As my mind raced with possible scenarios of what could have happened to my sister, I thought about what state of health I would find her in when I arrived. My thoughts darted so quickly that they triggered my emotions. I continued to have thoughts, such as, would I find that my sister had died when I arrived at the hospital? What if she never awakened from unconsciousness? I should have called her sooner. How would I tell my mother that her daughter was seriously ill and might die? All these thoughts raced through my mind in a seemingly uncontrollable way, until I decided to get control of my thoughts. I said to myself, out loud, "Stop this uncontrolled thinking—it is of no benefit to her *or* myself." Then I took a deep breath, and I decided to "take a step back" from my thoughts and emotions. In this way, I could now, by choice, be an observer of what was going on inside me. I found that I could now *choose* how I would stand in the unfoldment of the experience.

1

Finding Our Way

As human beings, we are far greater than we have known ourselves to be. The time to allow *all that we truly are* to come forth in our vast universe is now. I believe the key word is to "allow"—to allow all aspects of ourselves to become unified for our well-being and humanity. I have always believed that the only way to make a difference in life is to become all that I can be—to reach my fullest potential as a human being. We have heard from many that change in our lives begins from within, and then, over time, it manifests in our outer world. This concept of change is correct—however, the change we make in our lives that *I* am referring to, by means of *choice,* takes us one step closer to unification, or wholeness of Self, without attachment to outcome. It is not the same as "taking the high road" so that we can face our challenges in life better; rather, it's taking a higher view, or standing in a higher state of consciousness, secure in our "knowing," in the present moment.

I prefer *not* to use the word "challenges" as we decide to choose a new viewpoint, because, over time, this word has become a concept that sets up a duality—such as right or wrong, good or bad. The word "challenge" conjures up the idea that we need to battle *against* something or *overcome* a situation, when, in fact, all we need to do is *shift* out of our present state of awareness. When met with life "challenges," I tend to call them just what they are—experiences of life. Life experiences are nothing more than life moving along in its constant unfoldment and evolution; and each of us has a choice as to how we stand, or walk, in that unfoldment. By becoming *aware* that we have a choice in the way we experience any given moment, we empower ourselves to reach for another level of our true potential as human beings. This allows us to make different choices in life. How wonderful for *us,* that the time has come for us to allow ourselves to be all that we came to be—our true Selves.

Life is not easy at times, and it most definitely offers us a wide array of experiences. Unfortunately, from an early age, most of us are taught through the words or actions of others to be primarily reactive to life, rather than proactive. As children, it is rarely taught or modeled for us that there is another way of responding, or "Being," in any difficult life situation.

As I sat by my sister in the emergency room and wondered if she would regain consciousness, I found that I had before me an extraordinary opportunity to become an observer of the situation. I was able to say to myself, "Make a choice of how you want to be in this experience with your sister." Having contemplated and experimented with the following concepts prior to her collapse, I was able to stand more firmly in my convictions.

As I felt myself becoming an observer of this experience with my sister, I considered how I could respond. It was clear to me that I could respond emotionally; however, one lesson I had already learned throughout my life was that it is far better to respond *with emotion,* than to respond emotionally. By that I mean, as I sat in the emergency room with my sister, I showed empathy, and I was very caring as I tended to her needs—but I was not emotional. I chose not to allow myself the indulgence of *being* emotionally reactive, because when we respond in such a manner, it signals that we are making the experience *about us,* and not allowing it to be *just what it is.* Getting caught up in the emotionality of a situation tends to generate chaotic thoughts. It alters our physiology, thus creating mental and physical stress, and we end up perpetuating a vicious cycle of reactivity that does not benefit anyone.

I realized that if I kept running through all the scenarios that were darting through my mind, such as, "I should have contacted my sister sooner," or "what if she dies," that these thoughts would only lead to a never-ending loop of continued emotional responses. As I allowed myself to be an observer of the experience, I was allowing other aspects of the situation to unfold as they should. I was walking *in* the experience, but I was not *of* the situation. I was not allowing the situation to identify who I was. I did not know why my sister was having this experience, and I did not know why I was walking with her in it—I only knew that I was.

During that long night, as I sat next to my sister, my mind drifted to another aspect of myself that wanted to be heard. It was the part of me that wanted to pray to God to heal my sister. I knew of studies that showed how patients who were prayed for after cardiac surgery recovered quicker than those who had not been prayed for. However, I knew I did not want to plead with God for my sister's recovery, or assume that I even knew what to pray for in this situation. Honestly, I did not know if my sister should live or die.

I considered that if I prayed for her recovery, and it turned out to be incomplete, there was a possibility that she would require nursing-home care for the rest of her life. As I turned over such thoughts, I reconciled myself to the fact that *I had no idea* what the best outcome was. One thing I did know to do was to detach from any preconceived positive or negative outcome, and allow her situation to unfold as it should. I did affirm that my sister, and all who administered to her, were guided and directed by their higher Selves. When I speak of higher Self, I am referring to our next level of consciousness beyond our ego-based human consciousness, which is called Soul or Christ Consciousness. Our higher Self can avail itself of the wisdom of the Soul and the level of consciousness beyond our individual Soul, identified as a higher Presence, Intelligence, Source, or God. Our Soul houses its own wisdom as well the ability to interpret wisdom, of a higher state or stage of consciousness. Whereas, the outworking of any situation in our physical world is in relationship to our level of consciousness that we choose in any given moment. As I acknowledged that I was not in charge or in control of my sister's destiny, I sat back in a peaceful calm, while I tended to her needs and served as her advocate. I recognized that I was now able to be with my sister from a different place within myself, which was one of detachment from outcome—and within that detachment, I was free to be fully present with her.

It was very interesting to me that as I surrendered to a higher Presence, there was an indescribable peace and calmness that permeated the room. The nurses, doctors, and all that attended to my sister's physical and medical needs could not have been more attentive. After obtaining a sense of inner peace within myself, I suddenly had a thought, and I immediately sought out her doctor to give him additional information about my sister's health history. The doctor took the information I had given him, and then decided to order a new medication for her. As I reflected on the encounter with her doctor, it was interesting that not only was I able to find him, but that this busy doctor had time to speak with me. Shortly after, the nurse administered a new medication to my sister, and as the night progressed, it appeared that this medication served as the turning point in my sister's journey back to consciousness.

The broad concept I became aware of when I examined this experience was that *I have a choice* in how I perceive my life or any given situation. I realized that no two people have the same experience, even though it appears that in the situation, at least, they are interdependent and interconnected. I learned that I did not have to be reactive in a situation; rather, I could take a proactive approach, which originated from a different place within myself. It became very clear to me that outer factors or appearances did not have to influence my response to any given situation; instead, my inner knowing was now becoming my preferred response to any experience.

The experience with my sister rekindled a knowing that I have had since childhood. I can remember so clearly how, as a child, when I was confronted with any stressful or unpredictable situation, I instinctively knew to go within, before "going without" to do what I needed to do in the world. As a child, I always felt guided, protected, and directed in a very unusual way, and it was not until later in life that I understood why I felt as I did. As I grew older, I came to identify my childhood experience as being *in* the world, but not *of* the world. I was fortunate at a very early age to become aware of another aspect of myself that was always there for me, if I cared to listen to it—my higher Self. However, as time went on, because my inborn state of consciousness was not encouraged, it fell away, in some respects, as my primary mode of functioning in the world. I have since realized that it was that long night with my sister that reawakened and deepened my relationship with my higher Self. It has helped me to intellectualize concepts to describe my instinctive response of "Being," as experienced in my childhood.

My observed response and new awareness of my experience has allowed me to identify concepts that reflect a person's ability to transform or elevate a situation to a higher and more satisfactory level of consciousness. It was revealed to me that there exists a path to the doorway of a more satisfactory state of "Being," which can be applied to any life situation. I call this process, **"The Path to Knowing."**

The Four Steps of the Path to Knowing:

1. **Acknowledge** the situation *as it is.*

2. **Surrender all beliefs or ideas** you may have about the situation.

3. **Allow** that which is being revealed to you.

4. **Accept** that which is given to you, and trust that the guidance you receive from your greater Self is valid and reliable.

Let's look at each step more closely.

1. **Acknowledge** the situation *as it is.* Your opinions about the situation are not really going to change it, are they? No. *It is as it is.* Acknowledge that this particular situation *is just as it should be*—whether you approve of it or not—and that it if it was meant to be different, it would be. In my sister's case, since I had an awareness that the situation was as it should be, I was able to stand in the present moment, and not look backward or forward, searching for a potential solution that might have only created more chaos. By acknowledging what was before me, I was able to shore up my energy and prevent it from draining away in an attempt to make the situation something other than it was. It is a good practice throughout our busy day to periodically evaluate if we are fully present in the activity we are engaging in—or, are we present in body only, and not in soul? If we find that we are not fully present, we are able to consciously realign ourselves to Be in the moment by being passionate about where we are or what we are doing. Again, this comes full circle with the idea, "It is as it is." If

we *should* be experiencing something different in any given moment, we *would* be.

When we stand present, in the moment, we prevent our chaotic thoughts or feelings from intervening. Whatever may appear, if we can be present with it, and think "nothing" about it, we may find that just "being with it," and taking it at face value, is very freeing. In any given situation, when we can firmly claim, "It is as it is," we have now energetically detached from the situation, which is very different than taking a neutral stance or saying, "I really do not care what happens." Total detachment is having no thought about what is or what should be! Acknowledging the situation *as it is* takes consistent, conscious discipline and a practice of negotiating the mind. You will find that when you begin this first step, your mind will want to run rampant with thoughts and ideas of how things should be different. Therefore, we need to forego the will of the ego as we step into *It is as it is.*

2. **Surrender** all beliefs or ideas you may have about the situation. Stand firmly in place, knowing that there is a Presence and Power in charge, which is greater than your own ego personality. I believe the greatest obstacle to *surrendering* is controlling one's mental or body reactivity, and to avoid getting trapped in the random, fearful, repetitive, negative thoughts that fight to keep our attention. I believe we have given so much power to our mental capacity that it inhibits us from being able to allow the greater picture to unfold as it should. We have allowed our mental gymnastics to dictate our actions, as opposed to going within

for greater guidance and *allowing that guidance to flow through our minds into action*.

Knowing that there is a Presence and Power beyond our human ego is a personal belief or a conviction one may attest to. It may present as a sense or feeling that there is more to the human experience than appearances would lead us to believe. It may be the conscious acknowledgement of "knowing," while not understanding *why* you know or *where* such wisdom may originate from. Since the beginning of time, man has written or spoken of a Presence and Power greater than himself that is nontangible in its essence, yet can still be felt on some level of our humanness. Personally, I have always felt connected to something beyond my ego self, as a sense of inner peace beyond any understanding I could ever intellectually conceive of. If I only consider the conception of life, and the magnificent workings of the human body, I have to concede that there is a greater Intelligence that prevails over All That Is. I just cannot fathom the idea that we are born, we die, and we live no more, for I believe consciousness, which we are, is in a state of constant evolution. As humans, we surely could not have designed ourselves, for science has spent an eternity attempting to discern how our complex bodies function. As a scientist may only believe in what can scientifically be proven, a person on a deliberate spiritual path, having a belief in a greater Presence in his or her life, moves purposefully forward in faith. As I step forward in faith, I believe that our *true* life purpose is the evolution of consciousness individually and collectively, as we allow our "knowing" and a greater Presence to move through our lives in a meaningful way.

As humans, our primary guiding force has become our ego-based thoughts and emotions. I know, without a doubt, that it is time to allow a greater expression of Self to be the primary director in our lives and the "captain of our ships." Surrendering is the process of looking beyond present appearances to allow a solution, a new outcome, or inner guidance to come forth. Looking beyond the appearance is doing what needs to be done in the physical while choosing a different consciousness to do it with. It is looking beyond the consciousness that created the situation and choosing a renewed consciousness while having the current experience. It is not denying your experience of the moment; rather, it is a conscious shift to allow a different experience, as revealed by your higher Self.

What I have found most helpful in the process of surrendering is to not attempt to redirect or stop any rambling mental activity, but rather to watch these thoughts as they go by, without attaching myself to them. I tend to stand firm and tell my chattering thoughts to either get behind me or to go off and chatter somewhere else. I do not try to stop my random thoughts, nor do I engage with them. I have found that not engaging with my ego-based thoughts is usually very effective in allowing my Self to remain more fully in the moment. When we can be in the present moment and surrender, we are now allowing a greater wisdom to arise from our "inner silence." Our inner silence is a state of receptivity in which our mind is no longer actively thinking, as it allows a greater knowing to come forth to guide and direct us from a greater perspective. At times during this step of surrendering, I will affirm, and reaffirm if necessary, that "I know *without a doubt* that there is a greater Presence and Power in this moment, which I am open and receptive to." Then I quiet my mind and listen in a receptive state to what may be revealed to me or not in that moment of inner silence. There are many techniques and practices that are taught to help you learn to quiet your mind; however, the disciplined practice of "inner silence" tends to be an individual choice. You may simply begin this disciplined practice by taking 2 minutes, three times a day, to sit down, close your eyes, and focus on taking three deep breaths. As you do so, turn within and say, "I am here, I sit in peaceful silence." Then, just "allow."

One must realize that for most of us, our mental activity has become our conditioned response. As such, this process I have identified takes practice. We need to understand that our thoughts tend to track forward or backward in the search of information for a resolution, which disallows the power of the present moment to be revealed. As humans, we often perceive the situation at hand on the basis of past or projected future experiences. Only when we can truly surrender to a situation, *as it is,* do we then have the opportunity to see beyond appearances with a new vision. Looking beyond appearances is the most difficult thing to do as humans, because we are so visual and our senses are tied so strongly to our external world. We are constantly receiving feedback about our material world, even though we may think we are not.

To look beyond appearances is not to deny what has occurred, because as we have already stated in step 1, "It is as it is." Therefore, we have simply *moved beyond* appearances and stood firm in knowing that there is another way to walk in the situation. That which appears before us does not have to be as it appears. Many times, I will say to myself—as in the experience with my sister—"I hear what is being said, or I see what is being shown to me, but I know the Truth of the situation." I continue to reaffirm that "I stand with conviction, in knowing that this situation does not have to be as it appears, and that there is a higher Self and Presence in charge," as I allow the situation to unfold from a higher perspective

3. **Allow** that which is being revealed to you. Allowing is the third step in transforming one's state of consciousness to a higher state of "Being" as we walk through life. By achieving inner silence, we allow that which is being revealed to us to come forth in a new way. By not attempting to interfere with the natural course of events, our minds and bodies are now receptive vehicles to express our deeper sense of the situation. The inner guidance or knowing that is received during this time of silence is not fear or ego based, and it is only of the highest good. At this stage in our awareness, we have to resign our *personal* knowing, and allow and trust in our *greater* knowing. When we trust in the guidance we have received, then we can move forward and do what has been given to us to do. Our higher state of consciousness may occur as a knowing, a guidance, a nothingness, or just the experience of an "inner sense" that signals a connection has occurred. Any doing that we perform in the outside world is

done by trusting in the process—and by that I mean, trust without questioning. Many times when my mind is in a state of chaos and out of control with continual streams of thought, I will simply repeat to myself, "God is." When I affirm "God is," followed by no other words or thoughts, I gently become re-centered within myself and the rambling thoughts move away without effort. This exercise helps me to stay present as I shift within, to a state of silent receptivity as I wait.

Don't be disheartened if it takes time to evolve into allowing; for at this state of egoless consciousness, one's awareness is no longer intellectual, but experiential in nature. "Experiential" refers to the act of bearing witness to our inner silence, which allows the knowable unknown to come forth from our higher Self into our lives. The unfoldment of this step requires repeated self-discipline to sit in a state of inner silence and to trust in the knowing that comes forth, even though you're being confronted with a set of appearances that may not always match up with what your inner guidance tells you. This process of approaching the doorway to our higher Selves, and then moving through that doorway to sit in inner silence, takes continued choice and practice.

4. **Accept** that which is given to you, and trust that the guidance you receive from your greater Self is valid and reliable. This final step involves **acceptance** of that which is offered to you in silence, and being at peace with the presentation of it in your life. We must not waver in our "knowing" as we follow the guidance we received in our receptive state. We do what we have been guided to do, until we are instructed differently.

It is vital for our expansion of consciousness that we learn to stand with conviction in our truth. As we allow and accept our inner guidance to come forth, only then can we move in the guided direction.

This is one of my favorite Zen Buddhist stories, called "Maybe," which illustrates acceptance, without questioning that which is presented from our higher Self. This story also exemplifies how effortless our life can be as we walk in a state of higher Presence and trust.

There is a Taoist story of an old farmer who had worked his crops for many years. One day his horse ran away. Upon hearing the news, his neighbors came to visit. "Such bad luck," they said sympathetically.

"Maybe," the farmer replied. The next morning the horse returned, bringing with it three wild horses. "How wonderful," the neighbors exclaimed.

"Maybe," replied the old man. The following day, his son tried to ride one of the untamed horses, was thrown, and broke his leg. The neighbors again came to offer their sympathy on his misfortune. "Maybe," answered the farmer. The day after, military officials came to the village to draft young men into the army. Seeing that the son's leg was broken, they passed him by. The neighbors congratulated the farmer on how well things had turned out. "Maybe," said the farmer.[1]

So. Walking a different way in life, walking along the Path to Knowing, consists of acknowledging what is, surrendering any beliefs that your ego-based desires should ensue, allowing your higher Self to direct your life, and accepting and embracing the wisdom you are given in the moment. These outlined steps transform our mental and physical bodies to engage in our lives in a new and supportive way. The human mind and ego now become partners in the unfoldment of our greater Selves. As we evolve in consciousness, we express greater moments of clarity and insight, and become more readily aware of that which we are guided to do in the physical world, whenever we are faced with a particular situation.

After about a week of lying in a catatonic state, my sister regained full consciousness, and was eventually discharged to a nursing home for rehabilitation. I remember driving her home after her recovery. She asked me a series of questions: "What do you think is the purpose of life? Why are we here? Where do you think we go when we die? Are you afraid of death?"

I acknowledged the depth of her questions, reflecting that many have sought answers to them since the beginning of time. We discussed how a person can study the religions of the world and read the various philosophies on these topics, but that, eventually, one needs to find her own truth. I shared my ideas of my own personal truth about these questions, but I encouraged her to seek her own—whatever that truth may be. I told her I believed that our earthly experience in this life is a journey in the expansion of consciousness. I also pointed out that since she had asked these profound questions, her answers would come in a way that was unique to her life expression.

Over time, my sister regained her full function and had no memory of her unconscious episode. Although it was never determined what actually caused my sister's loss of consciousness, she did quite well for the following 3 years, until her sudden death in 2008.

2

It Is a Choice

As I touched on in the last chapter, we as humans tend to live an ego-based consciousness, which is a linear-based cause-and-effect reality. The ego is the part of our psyche that controls thought and behavior, and the part that is most affected by and in touch with external reality. Typically, we think or do something from our ego response mechanism and believe the cause of our experience to be outside of us. Then, when the cause creates an effect we do not like, we believe ourselves to be victims of this external effect! This level of consciousness represents a mental, emotional, physical, or spiritual response system that perpetuates itself. This system is devoid of the awareness that we cause our "reality of effect" by our reactivity. The reason I depicted the ego-driven human consciousness as a straight line, even though one might think it would be portrayed as circular, is because this process of thinking extends indefinitely into all areas of our lives, until we choose differently. This process of thinking or responding is without boundary and is superficial and one-dimensional. In this way, we will go on infinitely, without ending, while not interacting with the other aspects of our Self.

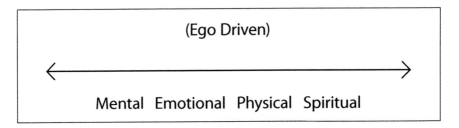

Along with collective human agreements ("misconceptions") such as these, we cycle through developed patterns of causal response in our lives over and over again, until something happens that makes us so uncomfortable that we seek outside intervention. Outside intervention can take a variety of forms, such as seeking help from a counselor or minister, to lashing out at others or indulging in drugs and alcohol. As you are aware, some personal interventions can have more of a positive effect on our well-being than others.

My personal experience is that repeating the same mental or emotional patterns, over and over again, gets us nowhere. It has been said that doing the same thing over and over, and expecting different results, is insanity (it certainly creates insanity!). I believe it is time to halt our self-induced insanity, and realize that no one is doing anything *to us* except for ourselves. Overcoming this pattern is a two-step process. The first step is to take responsibility for our own actions and experiences. Secondly, we must choose how we will respond to that which has shown up in our lives. Yes, I hear you when you say, "My parent or my spouse is doing this or that to me! And that is why I am this way or why I'm reacting the way I am." I can understand what you're feeling and experiencing, and I say to you, "Yes, but who is allowing the experience of another to be yours, but you?" I am aware that we are all interconnected, and sometimes we are interdependent, as well. However, the starting point in ending our insanity is examining more closely the mentality of "he said, she said," or "that it is his or her fault."

In this moment, surrounded by the very people and events you have in your life right now, you can take a stance and *choose how you want to walk in your world.* When someone is projecting anger, disappointment, or even hatred toward you, remember that it is usually a reflection of the one projecting—it is not about you at all. Let us start by trying to not take the experiences of others that are projected onto us personally. I realize this is easier said than done, but we have to start somewhere if we are ever going to experience any meaningful life change.

Just as my sister's emergency-room experience was about her, and not me, I had a choice in how I responded to my experience of it. I took ownership for my part in this experience, and my sister allowed her own experience. It seems to be a facet of human nature that as we observe someone else's pain or discomfort, we want to make it about us and not about them. We want to own that which is not ours through entanglement, rather than looking at what we are feeling or doing in the situation. We want to take on the other person's pain and suffering, as if it is really going to help the other person—but, as we all know, one cannot possibly know how another truly feels. Once we can acknowledge our part in any given situation, we can then go on to create our own experience from a place of awareness.

As we make the personal choice to grow and evolve in consciousness it is important to no longer react to the appearances of a situation, and choose instead to *be a witness* to appearances and then to *experience the situation from the perspective of our inside observer.* We must begin to look within ourselves for direction and answers, not to others or to the outside world. It is time to go within, to our inner wisdom, and then to "go without," to do, say, or be that which we sense as a greater knowing. The "cause" in our life should be Self-generated from a higher place of wisdom within ourselves, which is then allowed to be expressed in the creation of our own effect. We *become* the cause and the effect of our reality as we stand in our Truth and become our own creator, which is much greater than that generated by our ego-based personality. By doing so, we no longer allow our human-based ego, someone else's ego, or a situation to be our cause; thus, we become more fully the force that creates our effect. As put so well by Albert

Einstein, *"You cannot become free with the same consciousness that enslaved you,"* so let us choose differently in our life.[2]

During my years as an oncology nurse, I noticed that one of the most difficult things a patient with a cancer diagnosis had to face was how to redirect toward wellness. One patient might choose surgery, and no other treatment; another might choose all medical treatments available, while another might seek alternative medicinal options, and forego traditional medical treatment. Another might select prayer.

What I observed in each patient, after he or she worked through the initial shock and reaction to the diagnosis, is that each individual had to choose his own truth, for there was no right or wrong choice. He had to decide, from the core of his being, how he could direct his energy on a daily basis for his well-being. As we know, life is full of all degrees of decisions and choices; however, it usually is not until we are faced with some catastrophic event that we take the opportunity to reevaluate our personal stance in it all. Do we make a choice that is congruent with the core of our beings, or do we choose a purely reactive response, and one that might be expected of us? As with a patient diagnosed with cancer, we too have an opportunity to choose our truth from a greater place within ourselves; and, hopefully, it occurs under less trying circumstances.

Let me ask you this: Where does your well-being come from? Does it lie in another's truth, or is it an expression of *your* inner truth that leads to your well-being? For example, say you're standing in a coffee shop with a friend, and you're deciding what to order. With the wide variety of choices before you, do you allow your friend to choose for you? Will you be satisfied with what she orders, or would you rather select something for yourself? By making your own selection of what you'd like to eat or drink, you have now made a *conscious choice* on what you want in your dining experience. How could your friend know what your dietary restrictions might be or what your body might be craving to eat that day? If you allow yourself to express your truth or what you desire, you must know that it can only be for your highest good at your evolutionary stage of consciousness. If we had the advantage of seeing the grander universal picture, only then could we truly appreciate and understand why things are as they are. Although we usually cannot see the greater universal plan, we can, through the allowing of our greater individualized vision, live in a self-created universe of inner wisdom. Consider that our attainable level of consciousness tends to precede our experiences in life. Take hold, and start your journey into the discovery of the greater You—a You that you have always known, even though you may have allowed the world around you to tell you differently. I say to myself daily, "I welcome that greater *I* that I Am, to come forth every day, in every way, in my life, to guide, direct, and protect me."

When I was first married, one night my husband was late coming home from work, and he had not called me, which was very unusual. I recall the inner turmoil it created for me—for some unknown reason, I was angry and hurt, and yet concerned for his well-being all at the same time. This experience was a profound lesson for me, because I learned that night that what I was experiencing had *nothing to do with my husband,* who was always very timely and considerate. Rather, what I was experiencing was a recollection from my childhood, and I was projecting it onto him. I was projecting an old emotional memory onto my husband for something he had no responsibility for and did not even know about. When I was very young, my parents separated and then later divorced. It was during my early years that my father made arrangements to pick me up for some activity and was always late. He never called to tell me if his plans had changed. So very often, I would be left waiting for my father, wondering if he would ever show up, or if something had happened to him. We have all had experiences similar to mine, in which something occurs in our lives that leaves a lasting emotional impact. Then, we later transfer its impact to other situations, without the awareness of doing so. Hopefully, at some point in our lives, when our transference creates enough chaos, and we are able to view it as inappropriate, we can eventually ask ourselves, "What is going on within me to illicit the feeling or response that I am observing in this situation?"

Doing what I instinctively knew, the first thing I did in this experience was to become *aware of my uncomfortable feelings* that had arisen within me, and I owned them for what they were—an extension of my own misperceptions. The situation was as it was. It was because of my willingness to be aware of my self-created insanity that I realized my emotions were signaling to me that something was off within *my* experience. In that moment of clarity, I made a choice to experience this situation differently than appearances would have led me to believe.

In this experience with my husband, I *detached* from what was, and *surrendered* to the fact that I needed greater wisdom in the situation. I surrendered to that which I needed to know, be, or do; then, I *allowed* and *accepted* things to be different. My personality and ego took a back seat to my higher Self, as I declared that I no longer wanted to continue in this emotional pattern. As I acknowledged that there was another way to be in this moment of awareness, it was revealed to me. As I was freed to become an observer of the insanity my emotions were creating for me, I also was given the opportunity to create a new present moment. I acknowledged my past and present experiences for what they were—opportunities for me to grow. I then consciously let go of this old emotional pattern, which I had developed without even knowing it.

In my moment of choice, I could feel an inner shift, and a greater wisdom came forth from within. When my husband came home, I shared my awareness with him—and, thereafter, because of my conscious choice to respond differently, the previous emotional pattern lost its power to effect similar future experiences.

Do not be surprised if, as you engage in this process of awareness, your personality and ego appear front and center, trying to tell you that your decision to choose differently is absurd. As we evolve in consciousness, we come to realize that our ego's existence has been rooted in self-survival and preservation of our species. It often creates confusion in our lives, along with intense pain, suffering, and fear. The human ego does not always create negative outcomes, but it has produced different outcomes than we would prefer at times. As we begin to awaken, we move out of our survival state and find ourselves with a new choice regarding the functioning of our ego. Our ego does not have to be forgotten as we evolve in consciousness; rather, it must be shifted into a new supporting role, no longer functioning as our primary operating system.

As we begin to become aware of our ego responses, which are rooted in human consciousness, we start to awaken from what has been, to become aware of what is available to us as we *evolve in consciousness*. As we choose to evolve in consciousness either by desire or necessity, we choose a greater knowing. As we walk this path, we must continue to detach from our ego-based illusions that tell us we are different than we know ourselves to be. Even if we embark on a "spiritual journey," don't be fooled by the appearance of a wolf in sheepskins—the ego can disguise itself well.

If you are drawn to this book at this time in your life, you are in the process of evolving beyond a survival-based consciousness, and you are ready to be a creator and a co-creator of your reality. We may not like many of our past experiences, and we might find them hard to let go of, yet we must not continue to allow them to define who we are. Instead, we must acknowledge that we are much greater than the events of our chaotic past or our present experiences, and then consciously allow a new internal shift. *When we become attached to our experiences, or allow them to define who we are, the mind and ego are in charge—and we have lost touch with our true Self.*

Are these things I speak of straightforward, or easy to do? Is it as simple as waving a magic wand? As nice as that would be, the truth is, it takes much courage, discipline, and desire to shift to a new state of Being. *Being* refers to the state or quality of existence as one's essential nature (as defined according to the *American Heritage Dictionary*[3]). Whereas, our essential nature is our expression of our true Self, from an awareness of our Soul, or Christ Consciousness.

What we are seeking is what mankind has searched for since the beginning of time: Our true Self. And if your experience of your journey to Self is anything like mine, you may understand that it has always felt like something greater than your ego-based self has been propelling you forward. For some reason, I have always known that we do not have to live life by a series of default mechanisms we were shown early in life, and that there is another way to live this earthly experience. I have always been aware that, as individuals, we hold a greater truth and power within each of us than the collective human consciousness would want us to believe. On our human journey, we have often forgotten our greater truth, which will only become tangible when we begin to acknowledge it and allow its presence to be felt. We do not step onto the path of awakening and enlightenment for better things, or for a healing of some sort, but rather to reclaim that which we have always been. As we reclaim our true Self and live our potentiality, life begins to unfold in miraculous ways, with less personal effort and direction on our part.

I encourage you to take charge of your life experiences, and choose to walk differently in the world; that is, assuming that you are dissatisfied with your current lot in life. My suggestion is that, when you bump up against a situation in life, stop, take a deep breath, and step back for a moment to gain new clarity. Ask yourself, "From where does this experience originate?" or "Why must I be having this experience at this time in my life?" Wait for an answer, for it will come. Then, take ownership of whatever you are experiencing—do not attempt to project it onto another. Indeed, you must own it, because it is yours. Ask yourself, "Is this indicative of a pattern in my life that I would like to see changed?" and then go within, and ask for your inner guidance or wisdom to come forth.

I know that if you are reading this material, you are ready for a life change, and you are willing to take ownership of your experiences. You have a deep desire to stop having others or random life experiences dictate what you should be experiencing in any moment. You are no longer choosing to be reactive to your world—rather, you are deciding to become proactive, from the inside out.

Again, all of this requires a desire to take charge of your own life experiences and play by your own rules, not someone else's. As I said before, every situation "Is as it is," and if it was meant to be different, it would be. In knowing this, we are able to experience our current situation differently. There is an unspoken freedom that comes when we acknowledge that something "just is."

When we are no longer attached to a situation or its solution, and we are not trying to make it something that it is not, we open the door for our higher Self to come forth, to show us our highest good and the highest good of all concerned. It is then our job to let go, allow, and follow our inner guidance as it directs us on what to do in the moment. As we learn to control our wild thoughts and emotions, our minds and bodies can now become avenues for our higher Selves to express in any given experience. The past cannot be fixed or altered in any way that makes it correct or better—we can only acknowledge it, forgive ourselves for our misperception, and let it go as we shift into a new perception.

When I was a nursing student, I was on my way home from a late-night training session and sharing a conversation with a fellow student. We were talking about life in general, and my friend asked me, "What do you see for yourself, as we move forward after graduation?" I had just turned 21. I said to her, "My life is like an open book. I have realized that up to this point, my life was what others had taught me or dictated to me what they thought life should be. I can see now that life has been presented to me as it appeared from another's perspective, and that their way of living or perception of life was their truth, not mine." I told my friend, "I am in search of my own truth, whatever it may be—for however long it might take, I am committed to me."

In the words of Ralph Waldo Emerson:[4]

> *Be not a slave of your own past—plunge into the sublime seas, dive deep, and swim far, so you shall come back with self-respect. With new power, with an advanced experience, that shall explain and overlook the old.*

Life happens. Things happen to us that we do not like, and

sometimes, we feel powerless to change our lives. But I want you to know that, no matter what lands on your doorstep, you have the power within you to choose how you experience your life. No one can ever take your inner power away from you. It is yours—own it.

Little did I know that shortly after reading Emerson's words, "plunge into the sublime seas," I would have an opportunity for plunging into my own. A pipe broke in my kitchen, flooding the entire kitchen and filling the crawl space underneath with water!

This is an opportune time to clarify that when I say to always go within, before going without, it does not mean you should negate the immediate things that need to be done on the material level. When I found out that a pipe had broken, my immediate and first response was to locate the water main and shut it off. First, however, I needed to shut down the power to the house before my husband could safely go into the 4 feet of water in the crawl space to reach the main water valve. While this task of going into the frigid water was necessary and uncomfortable, it was the initial step that needed to be taken.

After the water was shut off, as you can imagine, my kitchen was a mess, and something needed to be done to get the water out. I was faced with yet another situation in which I had to decide how I wanted to handle it. I had to ask myself if I wanted to respond with anger and become the victim, asking, "Why me?"

Since I have consciously become aware that I have a choice as to how *I want to be* in any experience, I took a deep breath and implemented my steps of the "Path to Knowing." I immediately acknowledged that, "This situation is as it is, and is just as it should be." Saying this statement to myself allowed me to avoid getting angry or upset, and helped me shift to a different perspective. As I was able to acknowledge the situation as it was, I withdrew my energy from trying to make it different. I consciously surrendered to what was in the moment—not that I liked it!—and I then became the observer, trusting that my higher Self knew how to proceed.

It was very late on a Sunday night, so as I picked up the phone book, I knew that I would be guided to the perfect plumber to assist us. I allowed myself to be open and receptive to the help that I sought, and it came in the most helpful ways.

It took about 2 months for our home to be returned to its original state. The most unusual thing about the entire event was that when everything was repaired, and the kitchen was returned to its identical state before the broken pipe, nothing looked different. I was fortunate to have located the original carpenter, who had remodeled the kitchen only 3 years before, and he was presently between jobs and was more than happy to have the work. I was able to replace the ruined cabinets with identical ones from the same manufacturer, so the new cabinets matched the ones that had not been damaged. I was even able to reproduce the original countertops and flooring.

Going within before going without does not mean that we should abstain from taking action in the physical realm; rather, we are able to do so in a different way. Life tends to no longer happen *to us*—instead, with our inner guidance as our director, we allow life to unfold. Did I spend many hours reconstructing the home? Was I physically tired at times? Absolutely. But, I have to honestly say that when the project was completed, it had taken nothing of or from me. I was grateful for the wonderful people who assisted in the reconstruction. I had no attachment to the incident, so no pattern was created or added into my psyche to cause me some type of mental, emotional, or physical pain later on. In my conscious experience of the broken pipe, there was no anger or reminiscent frustration, no "why me," no thoughts lingering. It was over and done with on all levels of my being; it was an event that just happened.

My own experience with the broken pipe reminds me of this story: There is a great flood, and as the water is rising rapidly, there is a man hanging out of his home window, praying for God to rescue him. As a rescue boat comes by, the man is asked if he would like to get in, and he replies, "No, God will save me." The water continues to rise, so the man climbs to safety on the roof of his home. A rescue helicopter hovers overhead and offers to hoist him to safe ground. However, once again, the man says, "No, God will save me." The water rises higher, and the man drowns. When he gets to heaven, he says to God, "Why did you let me drown?" God replies, "I sent you a rowboat, and I sent you a helicopter. What more did you want?"

The moral of this story is that we never know where our good might come from, so we must remain open and receptive to the form that our higher Self sends forth.

When we are faced with a situation in life and a negative or even a positive emotional response comes up, it is signaling to us that we may need to stand back and examine where this emotion is coming from. I am not advising you to live without emotion—but living emotionally sends us on a downward spiral. The chaos of the world may be happening around you and even seem to be happening to you, but how you respond is totally up to you. When we can acknowledge that we do not like how a particular situation is making us feel, we know it is time to shift differently within it. It is time to choose a different operating system.

3

Knowing

It was sometime in February when I received a telephone call from my niece, who wanted an opportunity to come to Chicago with her 2-year-old son for a fresh start. After much family discussion, we decided to bring them into our home. Friends asked me, what was the plan for my niece and her child when they arrived? My consistent response to my friends and family was that I did not know, and that I would know what to do when I needed to. I can honestly tell you I had no preconceived ideas about how the situation with my niece would or should go, and I had no attachment to the outcome. All we were doing, as I would with my own children, was to give my niece an opportunity to change her life and the life of her son.

At the time, I had a house full of people—four generations living under one roof!—which was very interesting. When my niece arrived, her son was ill, so the first order of business was to secure health care for them both. We went through the necessary government channels. If, at any time, I had looked beyond the task at hand, and not stayed in the present moment, I most definitely would have been overwhelmed, and might have ended up operating and reacting from a fear-based state of mind.

My niece and I decided from the beginning that we would take each moment and experience it as it presented itself. Within 12 hours of their arrival, she had the necessary paperwork in place, and her son was seen at a nearby clinic. If you know the government system, this is an unusual event to have received the needed assistance for them both so quickly. Without asking, clothes were offered to my niece, and toys and clothes were given to her son, as well. After about 2 weeks, it was time for my niece to look for a job. So, with the baby in the car, we embarked on a search for employment.

After being out most of the day, driving her to different places to fill out applications, I stopped at one business on a hunch—and it ended up being the right place of employment for her! However, if she wanted the job, she needed to be at work the next morning for orientation, without exception. Knowing this contingency, my niece accepted the position, even though it presented some problems. The major issue was that I had to leave town the following morning, and we had no one to babysit her son. I will admit that, by this time, after driving her around all day in search of a job, and then at last finding one that necessitated immediate childcare, I was feeling a little tired and overwhelmed!

As I became aware of my feelings of overwhelm, I decided to take my niece and her son home. I told her I was going out for a drive to clear my head. The emotional response I was feeling was one of frustration—so, in that moment, I decided to stand firm and detach from what I thought or what I wanted the outcome to be. I stated to myself that, "It is what it is, and it is just as it should be in this moment." I acknowledged that the outcome was not a reflection of anyone or anything, and I accepted the situation for what it was.

Within seconds of affirming my stance, I suddenly had a thought to call someone I knew in the daycare business. Through her, a door opened, and my niece's son was able to start daycare the next morning. Within 12 hours, a job had been secured, and her son enrolled in daycare, with all the necessary paperwork in place. By not attaching to any outcome, we allowed the next step to unfold in an orderly fashion. We followed the next step, and then the next step, until the situation had been fully resolved. As we surrendered, we allowed the perfect unfoldment of the situation to be revealed to us.

Can you imagine what would have occurred if had I pressed on in frustration and lashed out at my niece, rather than choosing to listen to my higher guidance? First of all, I would have projected my emotional reactions onto my niece, thereby not owning my feelings, which would have only created chaos and blame. Instead, I made a conscious choice in how I wanted to walk in this situation, which was in clarity and with a higher sense of knowing what to do.

Our higher knowing is available to us all, if we only have the courage and discipline to allow it to reveal itself. If we are able to realize and accept that our inner knowing is our long-lost best friend, then we can finally welcome it back into our lives. As humans, we tend to perceive our experiences as things that happen *to us,* rather than *because of us.* And so, as we live life unconsciously, we become victims of our life events. This does not allow us to take responsibility for our personal self, or, ultimately, that which we experience in life.

There is a story that goes something like this (which I have interpreted loosely): The creator asks, "Where should we hide man's greatest truth?" One angel responds, "We should hide it on the highest mountaintop." The creator responds, "No, man will persevere and find it there—that's way too easy." Another angel responds by saying, "We should hide it in the deepest depths of the ocean," and the creator responds, "No, not good enough. Man loves to explore his outer world, and he will find it there." After much debate, the creator says, "I know just where we should hide the greatest power of man—and that is within mankind itself. They will never look for it there." The creator was absolutely correct in his inference; looking within for his higher knowing or true Self is the last place mankind would look!

In the history of our race, we have almost never been taught or directed to go within to find the truth for ourselves. That which lies *within* houses the greatest knowing of all—our higher Self. I ask you, from where could your greatest guidance come from, other than within the depths of our own soul? We climb to the mountaintops, explore outer space, and dive to the depths of the sea in search of a challenge, or in search of happiness. However, if we would allow that which lies within us to come forth, our outer world and our life experiences would be transformed into expressions of peace, joy, and magnificence.

After a time, I realized that my niece was getting antsy living with us and wanted a place of her own. Acknowledging what I was feeling, I asked my niece to confirm my suspicions, which she did. And so, the journey began to locate a place for her to live. Numerous phone calls were made, apartments were toured, and helpful agencies were contacted. However, nothing seemed to come together for my niece and her son.

So, without attachment, and by surrendering to the situation, we continued to move forward in the process of obtaining housing. My niece had applied to a nonprofit county organization for assistance, and was initially declined; however, a couple of weeks later, out of the blue, we received a telephone call indicating that when an apartment became available, it could be hers, if she so desired. My niece agreed to the terms of the contract, which came with a slight reduction in rent, and she readied herself to move into the apartment when it became vacant. She also received help from another nonprofit community organization, which provided her first month's rent and security deposit. The location of the apartment was perfect for the two of them, only 1 mile from our home. Her son's daycare location was within walking distance from the apartment, and her place of employment was only 2 miles away. Without asking anyone, furniture began to flow to her. Even before she could move into the apartment, the way was revealed.

There is a principle in quantum science, which states that an atom can exist in more than one place at any given time, and that it is the observer who determines where the atom is to be found. When I apply this knowing to our opportunity to choose how we want to walk in our world, it all makes sense to me. If, in any given experience, we respond emotionally, with either fear or anger, as an example, we have now locked in our possibilities at that level of awareness. And if we make our experience about another rather than about ourselves, we have lost all power in the situation and have turned our destiny over to the domain of another observer.

However, if we can (a) acknowledge our initial reaction to any given experience, (b) not condemn ourselves for our reaction, (c) step back, and (d) take a deep breath, we can redirect. As we make the choice to stand firm with the knowing that what lies within us is up to the task at hand (indeed, more so than our chaotic mind and ego might ever be), *then* we are *on our way*.

So, as the atom can exist in multiple places at any given time, our proactive position that comes from within us can make multiple possibilities available to us at any given time. As quantum science tells us, it is the observer who locks in the position of the atom. In a similar way, it is our inner observer who can present a solution to us that we could never have considered possible. When we stand in a place of detachment, accepting that "It is as it is," the mind works with our inner knowing to lock in the new possibility as we move forward in our outer world. As our new possibility is reflective of our present level of consciousness we can move forward as we choose, for we always have free will of choice in any given moment.

I envision our higher Self as having the capability to survey all possible outcomes, to consider everyone concerned, and to assess our level of personal growth as it assembles or develops a greater plan. And it is within this process of allowing our higher Self to guide us that we have ascended to our potentiality as a human being. We have gone within—and not to the outer world—for our truth, direction, and guidance. Our decision, action, or knowing now becomes a product of our detachment. Without this detachment, our decision might be based on fear or greed or egocentric in nature and only create more chaos in our lives than we bargained for. By committing to choose the way you want to walk in *your* world, not *someone else's* world, you have empowered yourself beyond measurable means. Your inner world now becomes your cause and effect, and it presents itself in your outer world as an unfoldment from within.

In my relationship with my niece, as she began the process of starting a new life, I tried to show her a different way to walk in life. As time went on, she started to call me her "lucky penny," which we laughed about, as I really did not know how to respond to such a comment. It was not until much later, when I began to slowly remove myself from her day-to-day activity, that I realized how she correctly interpreted my presence in her life as her lucky penny. While I thought I was teaching her to become more self-guided and self-directed, she had not internalized anything I had tried to show her. When I walked away, everything crumbled. I realized that, in terms of consciousness, I was holding the door open for her. She was not able to keep the door open on her own, or maintain the same level of consciousness that was required to walk differently in her life.

In retrospect, I learned a most valuable lesson with regard to my supposedly supportive relationship with my niece. I realized that we might be able to lead someone to the doorway of his or her higher Self, but it is only through a commitment to their evolution in consciousness that they can pass through that doorway. I considered just how many times a practitioner or a healer supports a client at a higher level of consciousness, only for them to fall back, over time, into the same state of consciousness that created the situation in the first place. I wondered how many people experienced some type of healing with regard to a particular issue, to only replace it with a similar issue as time went on. I had to ask myself, What really constitutes a successful healing—is it the immediate effect in the outside world? Or, is it measured in consciousness?

As the story of my niece continued to change, so did my life and my awareness of my greater Self, which I grew to know better as time went on.

My niece had come to live with us in the beginning of April. By the end of April, my mother-in-law, Roselyn, who was terminally ill, had decided that she did not want any additional medical treatment and wanted to enroll in hospice. My husband and I fully supported her decision and went to her hometown to meet with her hospice personnel. Upon our arrival at her home, she met us at the door with her bags in hand and said she was going home with us—she wanted to live out her final days in our home. My husband and I respected her decision, and she knew we would do whatever was needed to support her.

I thought to myself that Roselyn's timing was so interesting—for when we brought her home, we would have two 80-year-old women living with us (my own mother lived with us at the time), our 16-year-old son, our 14-year-old daughter, my 30-year-old niece, her 2-year-old son, and my husband and myself—all under one roof! Initially, I felt somewhat overwhelmed and anxious by this arrangement. However, I knew this was only another step of my journey, and I was committed to what I believe is our potentiality as humans—so I forged on. There was a lot to juggle and a lot of needs to be met for many people, and at times I wondered if I was up to the task.

Having been a hospice nurse, I was curious as to how I would handle the experience of being "on the other side" of supporting a loved one during their declining days. I knew I was very good at telling, showing, and problem-solving for hospice families, but now I was participating in a very different way. I knew what it takes to support a family member in their hospice decision from observing other families, and I was about to experience first-hand what I thought I knew.

Again, I made a choice—I could allow my rambling mind and emotions to take over and create chaos, or I could stand firm, on holy ground in the truth of my Being. I took a deep breath and affirmed that the situation "Is as it is." I *acknowledged* my initial feelings, but did not attach to them, nor did I feel badly about experiencing them. I *surrendered* to the situation and remained open and willing for my higher Self to guide and direct me in this experience. I committed to *allowing* the unknown to come forth, and then *accepted* what was to unfold in any given moment. I committed to allowing my direction and guidance to come from a greater place within my Self, which I identify as Soul.

After standing firm, I stepped out into the outer world to make the necessary arrangements to bring Roselyn to our home that same evening.

4

Embracing the Knowing

In our human consciousness, we repeat the same patterns of behavior over and over again, which is a vicious cycle to nowhere. Amazingly, we ask ourselves, "Why me?" and complain that our life does not change. This continued way of functioning tends to create tremendous pain and suffering, whether we experience it as self-induced or perceive it to be induced by another.

This discomfort is created from us wanting and expecting things to be different than they appear in the moment. We have learned, not by any fault of our own, to be reactive rather than proactive in our lives. The constant repetition of behavioral patterns, whether we have the ability to identify the patterns or not, is what creates insanity. The linear-based system of response that we learned is one based on primordial survival, fight or flight. Don't get me wrong, fight or flight is a good tool to have if a train is fast approaching your car and you're stalled out on the tracks. In this scenario, obviously, you should get out of the car and run!

However, let me ask you this: If we led, for the most part, an inner-directed and guided life, is it *possible* we might not have even been on those tracks in the first place? Maybe your car, if it was going to stall, might have stalled out in your own driveway. Ponder this thought and possibility for a moment!

As my home filled up with people and medical equipment, I continued to stand firm in the knowing and experiencing of my inner guidance. Did I falter in my conviction at times? Absolutely! And yet, I learned to forgive myself and start all over again.

It was because of my conflicted relationship with my sister that I learned to begin again, over and over. Through the years, my sister and I had different viewpoints about a variety of issues. We had different approaches and perceptions of life—neither better nor more correct than the other. So many times I would have an encounter with my sister, and we ended up arguing, and then immediately afterward, I shook my head in amazement of the craziness that just occurred. I continually walked away from an encounter with my sister and resolved to take responsibility for my own contribution. Eventually, through choice and practice, I no longer reacted to her projection onto me, nor did I project onto her. I examined the emotions and reactions that were coming up for me in our encounters, and I owned them for what they were, as I let them go.

Sometimes, I was able to know where my uncomfortable feelings were coming from; other times, I did not. It really did not matter where they were coming from at this point in my knowing—all I knew was that I did not want to continue with the lifelong emotional pattern that was occurring between the two of us. I did not try to change my sister's behavior, because I realized that the choice to change was about me—not her.

One can spend years and years wading around in the emotionality of life, but at some point, we can consciously choose to stop being a victim, to take responsibility for ourselves, and to find empowerment from within. Sometimes we need to let go of what has been, and shift to a new way of being or become our new awareness. Uncovering our wounds and wallowing around in them will never change them. No matter how long we wait for vindication from the one we perceive to have inflicted the wounds on us, it will never come. The only person keeping our wounds alive is ourselves. The only one perpetuating the repetitive cyclical patterns created by our perceived wounds is *us!*

In my relationship with my sister, I consciously made a choice to exist in our relationship differently. When it came to settling issues between us, I did not want me to be right and her to be wrong. There was no trying to change my sister—I finally realized that her life and her journey were hers, and mine were mine, and that I could choose differently when it came to relating to her.

As I continued with my own inner work, over time, I became less judgmental of my sister, more loving, and more present with her. Could I have walked away from my relationship with my sister? I could have, but I chose not to, and honestly, I never even entertained the idea. However, I use my relationship with her as an example, to make the point that we always have the choice of free will in any situation. We may have a greater knowing about something, and choose not to listen as we revert to our old ways of reactivity. We may be aware that we have some life lesson to learn and decide not to face it until it almost knocks us down—for "free will" always reigns. Over time, I could be with my sister, no matter what, and do whatever was necessary to support her without it taking anything from or of me. I became detached from making her experience about me or my own life experience, and I allowed her to be herself. I learned so much as I witnessed the beauty and innocence of her existence. My new way of being with my sister was so freeing, I was just in awe as time went on. And now, looking back, I am so grateful that I chose to be with my sister in a different way—for neither of us knew then that we did not have much more time together.

Did I regress, at times, to my previous way of interacting with my sister? Yes, I absolutely did. However, the regressions became less frequent, and I caught them sooner. I began to see the craziness of my old ways of reactivity and self-denial in a new light. My conscious choice to walk in a different way with my sister gave me plenty of opportunities to practice my new way of Being, over and over again. It took work on my part to change, and since my old way of functioning only made me crazy, I saw no other option but to move forward.

At some point in your life, you may find that if you let go of the "he-said, she-said, he-did, she-did" type of reality and start anew with a different way of perceiving and processing life, you will be free in ways you could never have imagined. In reality, we cannot change the past. Moreover, as we have brought the past forward into the present, we have altered it so many times in our minds that it is no longer what it was in the first place! So where does the reality of any given situation lie, if, in bringing it forward into the present, it has now been changed? Let us no longer waste time trying to change the past. All we can do is become aware of the present and shift into a new way of Being.

Eventually, my niece moved into her apartment, and Roselyn became my primary focus. When she first received her terminal diagnosis, I had willingly promised her that I would support her on her journey of well-being, no matter what turn it might take.

As she grew more ill, I continued to implement the principles outlined in this book on a daily basis. There were mornings when she woke up, stating, "I guess I am still here—and I do *not* know why." My response to her, which is the same response I would offer to any seeker, is that, "It will be revealed to you at the appropriate time." I knew that the awareness of asking, in itself, would bring the answer forward. As time went on, Roselyn received answers in a variety of ways. Our motto became, "It is as it is, and is just as it should be." Repeating our motto freed us both—it released her from the self-imposed guilt and perception of being a burden to myself and the family, and it freed me from wondering why I was walking this path with her and having this experience.

Roselyn was a courageous woman. She never entertained the idea, "why me," or allowed herself to adopt a victim mentality. She allowed her greater knowing or truth to guide and direct her, when she sincerely asked, "Why am I still here?" As she progressed in her life review, for the first time, in many instances, she saw her life for what it really was: an amalgamation of misconceptions, which is natural enough for any human being. She became an observer of her life events, and saw her life play before her like a movie as she reviewed it. She became a witness of self-created insanity, something we all do in our humanness.

As time went on, her veil of separation fell, and she became aware of our human insanity, and our inhumanity to mankind. I was privileged to witness her awakening, for she shared so much with me. She taught me about surrendering to what was, and in her surrendering I watched her settle into a new peace. She allowed the way to be shown to her, and then accepted what was presented to her. She became grateful for her life experiences in a new way, and forgave that which she had misunderstood or had no control over. I witnessed Roselyn dying on multiple levels—in her emotional life, as well as in her physical life. She was allowing the illusions of life to fall away.

Like Roselyn, we all have an opportunity, daily, to allow false appearances to die away as we move forward in reclaiming our true Self. To "die" daily is to become aware of our emotional or mental patterns that no longer serve our well-being and then to have the courage to choose differently. If we resolve to accept the premise that we could have done better at times in our lives, then, within that knowing, we can forgive ourselves. We must forgive ourselves for past mistakes, for I will assure you that, if you had known better, you would have done better.

As Roselyn's physical health deteriorated, she had healing dreams—dreams of reclaiming the part of her that she had lost so long ago, but had never forgotten. She reclaimed her higher Self, which had now become a tangible inner sense of knowing. We all have moments in our lives, as Roselyn did, when we become aware of our greater Self. My offering to you, as well as to myself, is to allow these moments of awareness to occur more frequently. By becoming the observer of our everyday misperceptions, only then can we choose a truly different way of walking in the world.

If I had not embraced what was, when I was presented with

Roselyn coming to stay with us until she died, I would have missed the wonderful gifts she bestowed upon me. If I had not acknowledged, "It is as it is," surrendered to my higher Self to help me handle the situation, and then allowed and accepted what was presented to me, I might not have had such a meaningful, positive experience.

In her final weeks, Roselyn's veils of humanness became even thinner, and on one occasion, she shared with me that she saw her grandmother standing next to her bed and felt comforted by her loving presence. She shared with me the music she literally heard coming from the place she knew she was going to when she died. As I listened to what she was telling me, I knew she was almost home, in more ways than one. In the end, Roselyn had traveled a courageous journey back home, and she was now free.

5

Experiencing and Living Our Truth

As we practice being an observer and witnessing our own created insanity, and can let go of that which we no longer desire to experience; we are beginning to embark on the journey to live our truth. We may be feeling happy and content with our life as we evolve. We may decide that our world is good, and that it is working well. But allow me to ask you this: Does your happiness and contentment come from that which lies outside of yourself, rather from that which lies within? We all know someone who has all the latest gadgets, a bigger house, or the newest car, or who takes many vacations each year. By all appearances, they have it all. But do they really have it all? One never knows what really goes on in another's home, let alone within one's innermost self. What if your circumstances changed—would you still be happy? Don't get me wrong, happiness and contentment are worthy desires. Material possessions and life experiences are wonderful to have and enjoy. However, I believe it is important, as we continue to evolve in consciousness, to evaluate whether our happiness is dependent upon our external world working well. I believe that, periodically, we should evaluate *if we own* our desires and possessions, or *if our desires and possessions own us.*

If I consider my experience of happiness and contentment, it tends to be my outer experience that creates it or brings it to me—it does not originate from within. Joy and peace, however, reside in and bubble up from the depths of my *Soul*. And once joy and peace bubble up from within, they cannot help but be expressed in my outer world in a grand and self-created way. If my higher Self expresses in material ways, and if those material items are suddenly removed, there is no loss, because it was created from within and thus can be recreated again. Once I learn to live my life from within before I live it without, I have now become the *creator* of my life experience and all that resides within that spectrum.

The word *soul* has been tossed around in many different contexts. We have heard expressions like *soul mate, soul partner, soul music, soul food,* and *soul train.* Since the beginning of time, human beings have used the word *soul* in poems, writings, and music, but have we ever stopped to wonder what is really being conveyed when the word *soul* is used in everyday speech?

I am sure you have heard the words "heart and soul" used in a variety of ways. Someone might say, "This is the heart and soul of my work," or "I put my heart and soul into this relationship." The words *heart* and *soul* belong together because we access our souls through our hearts, and with our hearts open, we can experience our true Self, our higher Self. Have you ever noticed that when someone is truly compassionate, loving, or caring about their work, that they are able to do extraordinary things? If you read the biography of any great inventor, scientist, musician, artist, or poet, you will quickly realize that they were able to tap into some higher aspect of themselves to bring forth wonderful works of expression.

As humans, we have always known, on some level, of the greatness that lies within ourselves—our Soul. I invite you to allow that which you already are and have ever been to be expressed in a most exquisite way as you walk in your world. As you walk in a soulful way, you cannot help but make a difference in your own life, as well as in the lives of those around you. Like the inventor, scientist, or artist, as we become passionate about life and start living every day from within, the expressions of life that flow through us will be extraordinary.

This new way of walking in the world does not negate any obligations or responsibilities we have with regard to ourselves or others. Instead, all needs tend to be met in a very different way. As life begins to take on a different meaning, you now make your children's lunches from a place of deeper love, and the lawn is mowed with the joy of being outside in nature. Opportunities become an avenue of expression, and disappointments or unwanted experiences become a chance for personal growth to unfold. You may be thinking, as I have, "Let's just forget or bypass the personal growth part!" To which I say, "It is as it is, and is just as it should be." Life appears painful at times, but now we have new tools to help us evolve in consciousness as our lives expand.

The way of walking in the world that I have discussed is not magical, nor is it some form of positive thinking. Rather, it is a way of Being. In this way of Being, life begins to happen not to you, but from you—and life becomes a choice—your choice. You no longer attract wanted things to you, which your mind or ego thinks should be yours—instead, you now allow that which lies within you to become your outer expression. This outer expression may be your dream job or a new relationship that you have yearned for. The important thing is that it now originates *from your Soul,* not your ego. Remember the old saying, "Even before you ask, it is given unto you." Believe it, for it's the truth. As we now begin to be guided and directed from a higher place within ourselves, our causal Self unfolds in the outer world, uninhibited, as it is meant to do. The world I speak of is not one of survival or of getting, but one of self-expression and self-direction from your higher Self.

The Soul does not operate according to any laws of attraction; rather, it expresses *through* you, into form or an expression. The Soul does not draw our good to us, for it is *already* our good. As we claim the Self of our Soul, this vibration or cause creates and births its effect into form. As an analogy, it's like water transforming into ice—it represents an energetic change from one state to another, while still maintaining the same molecular composition.

The Soul is not seated in religion. Everyone has one, and everyone's is unique. If your Soul could speak, it might say, "Lay your personality and ego aside and commune with me—allow me to emerge and become your essence."

Now, instead of a linear type of human existence, which is based upon reactivity, survival, and emotionality, we move to an experience of Being, and living our true Self—our Soul consciousness. We go from an experience that resembles this—

Mental Emotional Physical Spiritual

an ego-based reality—to one like this—

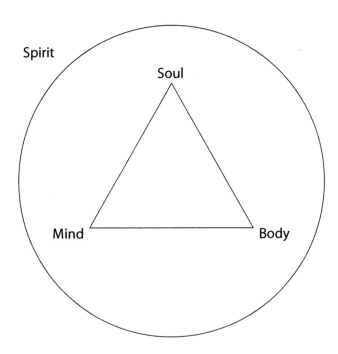

an experience that is Soul-based in nature, reflecting our commitment to begin to live soulfully.

This awareness of Soul arises from conscious choice and takes place through a continual desire to not only live, but to experience life differently than before. I believe that our true purpose in life is the constant expansion of our Beingness, as we continually evolve in consciousness. We can live a life in which the ego is the captain of our ship, or we can live a life that originates from the Soul—which I call, *living soulfully*. Again, it is a choice of how you want to walk in your world. Living an ego-based existence is probably an *easier* route to take, because, for the most part, it is what has been modeled to us for most of our lives. By default, we tend to mimic that which we have been shown to be a human truth. Take a look at your personal world and the collective outside world, and tell me what you primarily see as you become an observer. Even those individuals that seem loving, kind, and caring can be less than they appear if their giving is ego-based in nature.

The representation of our ego's expression in the outside world is *less than we really are*, whereas our Soul exemplifies *all that we have ever been and will ever be*. The Soul has the capacity to know all and be all, because the Soul is our connection to Infinite Intelligence, Source, or God—as well as an expression in our outer world. Source is the All-Knowing, and Spirit (depicted in the diagram) is the life force that animates our lives through all that exists. Consciousness, at any level, is simply the awareness of knowing. As Consciousness, we can be the observer *and* that which is observed; as the observer, I experience the observing, as well as that which is observed. Our existence is a cause-and-effect reality, and, ultimately, through different states and stages of consciousness, our causes and effects shift.

For the most part, many of us have spent our lives climbing (or crawling) up to the top of Maslow's pyramid of the hierarchy of human needs, to a level of self-actualization.[5] Depending on whose definition you study, self-actualization can mean a variety of things; however, I interpret it to be a high level of functioning in human consciousness.

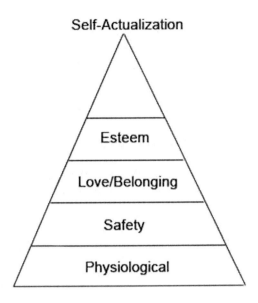

According to this model, in our human consciousness, our goal of self-preservation is the fulfillment of the hierarchy of needs: We are fed, safe, and loved, we feel good about ourselves, and we consider our actions to be ethical and moral. How much better could we be than this? We have worked hard, and we have successfully made our way to the top of Maslow's list. And then, one day, we may find that we feel empty inside, like something is missing. We might ask ourselves, "Is this all there is?" As we have climbed up this ladder to self-actualization, many people have incorporated some form of spirituality into their lives, which helps identify and make sense of one's life purpose—but, yet again, one may find that the chosen expression of spirituality is still not enough.

I believe that we feel empty inside because we have lived life from the outside in, not from the inside out. When you live life from the inside out, you never feel alone. When you become aligned with your soul, you cannot not help but feel guided, directed, and protected, and always in the right place at the right time. Your life takes on a life of its own and flows in an unbelievable way. As one lives soulfully, joy and peace exude from within and shine out into the world.

As we complete our survival-based human consciousness, we become aware of it for what it is—a primarily egotistic, insane existence. Upon witnessing the truth, we may experience grief and disbelief, which can ultimately propel us in search of another way of being in the world.

Our *awakening* occurs as we become the observer of our self-induced insanity and our limitations as humans. Upon our awakening, we begin to remember our true nature, and then we become truly free to choose another path. Be grateful for the unveiling of the purpose and reality of the human consciousness, for it reveals a new doorway. It is important to note that as we move from one level of consciousness to another, there has been no failure, but rather a completion of the consciousness we are expanding beyond. And so, our success is measured in our completion, not in how well we did while we existed in it. In this way, we can let go of any "should have, could have" regrets.

Do we have experiences in which we function at a human consciousness level, and then, in another moment, experience our Soul consciousness instead? Yes! We can shift from one level of consciousness to another in any given moment. However, as we continue to evolve our preferred state of consciousness by means of choice, we move into our Soul consciousness more frequently.

Is what I am describing to you simply wishful thinking, or does it seem like an impossibility? Know that soulful living is not a far-reaching concept—in fact, it is closer to you than your own breath. It is within you already, and always has been. So, now that you have been awakened to your true state of consciousness, it becomes a choice of how you want to exist in your life. Breathe freely in the truth of who you really are.

Our awakening out of a human consciousness level is akin to Michelangelo's sculpture of David. This sculpture was created on the basis of a vision or concept within the mind's eye of the sculptor, Michelangelo. For Michelangelo, the image of David already existed in the block of marble he was working on. Like Michelangelo, we chip away at that which we are not, to find who we really are—and in doing so, we unearth a magnificent aspect of ourselves—our Soul. As we strip away that which no longer serves us or that which causes us pain, we gradually reclaim our true Selves. With great desire and propulsion from our Soul, we keep moving forward, until one day, like Michelangelo's David, our sculpture emerges in all its magnificence. As the block of marble transformed into David, through Michelangelo's tireless efforts, we, through our unwavering efforts and eventual awakening to what is, *become the potentiality of our Soul.*

Just as Michelangelo began to reveal David, who lay within the stone, we embark upon our own journey to uncover and reclaim our true Self—that greater, individualized intelligence that exists within us and in all things. As Michelangelo envisioned that his sculpture lay within the stone, we must also move forward with the knowing that we will incrementally reveal our greater Self and allow it to be expressed.

As you probably have heard it said, all you need is a little faith, no more than the size of a mustard seed, and all shall be given to those that persevere, even in times of tribulation. In this way, I say to you: Have faith in the potentiality of your true nature, and in the knowing that it will be revealed to you at the appropriate time. The seed of our true natures resides in each and every one of us, and it is the desire of that seed of the Soul to *be that which it has come to be.*

As an apple seed's potential is to blossom into a fruit-bearing apple tree, it is our Soul's desire to reveal our higher Self as we expand in Soul consciousness. What the apple seed and our Souls have in common is that within both lies an intelligence, from which all potential arises. Our faith need be nothing more than knowing, without question, that an apple seed will bear apples, just as an orange seed will one day bear oranges.

This intelligent life force has proven itself to reside in nature, even in the tiny casing of an apple seed. How could it not reside within us? As we surrender and allow this intelligence—our higher Self—to express through us, we will experience the magnificent potentiality of our expression as human beings. Consider that Michelangelo must have had tremendous faith in the potential of his vision, for it took him 4 years to complete David. Michelangelo would not have been able to create the masterpiece he created, unless he allowed the higher intelligence within to work through him. Did he throw down his tools and walk away if he got frustrated? Did he give up on the whole sculpture, second-guess himself, or blame himself and others for tribulations along the way? We will never know what inner dialogue he may have had; however, we do know by the results of his magnificent sculpture that he persevered.

I am sure you have heard at one time or another that we are not human beings having a spiritual experience—rather, we are spiritual beings having a human experience. Within each of us, deep in our core, resides an invisible and scientifically unexplainable life force that desires to burst forth as our Soul's expression. As each apple seed blossoms into a tree, bursting with individual, unique apples, our individualized seed of our Souls bursts forth as a unique and individualized Soul expression. Just as no two apples are the same, no two souls are the same, in either appearance or expression.

I firmly believe that every soul fits, in a purposeful and individualized way, into the greater expansion of consciousness. Each soul serves as a piece of the puzzle, unique in itself and necessary in the evolution of universal consciousness. Whereas the universal soul is composed of all individual human souls, as an individual human soul, each of us comprises All That Is of the universal soul. In our essence, this makes us all One. As we are One, we are also One with all things. And as we are One with all things, we are, and always have been, All That Is.

6

The Road Is Narrow and the Way Is Straight

To live soulfully, it must be realized that the way is narrow and straight, and that it takes courage, commitment, and determination to reclaim our true Self. As we all know, the path is forgiving, as long as we are willing to pick ourselves up and begin anew as each opportunity presents itself. There is an old saying, that if you know more, more is expected of you—so as we grow and evolve in consciousness, we cannot go back to old ways of functioning, because they will no longer work. As we evolve in consciousness, we will consistently be offered an opportunity each day to allow our old ways to die away. Our desire to embrace a new way of being in the world will facilitate change. Now that we have become aware of and awakened to the human level of consciousness, we have the ability to shift out of our conditioned, egocentric behavior and reactions. During this process of awareness and awakening, it is also important to forgive ourselves for past and present regressions and to see them for what they are—an unconscious separation from Infinite Intelligence, Source, or God. This unconscious separation may also be considered a hypnotic state of humanness as we experience a lack of Oneness. If we do not forgive ourselves for our ignorance and let go of the attachment to prior situations, we will only create karma for ourselves, a "redo" of some aspect of our human experience that we cannot accept as being "as it is." Because we cannot let go of it and we want to fix it, we recreate a similar experience in hopes of finding some resolution. So when we cannot let go of the past, it becomes our fate, or destiny, at some point in our future.

As you awaken, do not be surprised at the length of time it can take to strip away the layers in this process of developing your new awareness. The human ego can take on a multitude of disguises. Just when you think you have shifted to living differently, something unexpected will occur to throw you off your center, and you will have to begin again. As I have been working through my own process, I've found it most interesting that some areas of my life are easier to strip away than others. For some, the issues associated with their health might keep triggering their emotional patterns. For others, their financial world has no triggers, and they can easily walk into a new way of being with regard to money. However, I assure you that as time goes by, your desire to live in a new way will become more prominent in your everyday life and will become your chosen response.

I have often asked myself, "Can I live the way I have been describing *all the time?"* While I'm not sure I can do it *all* the time, I will never say it is not possible. We tend to be so entrenched in our material world, with its endless responsibilities, that when you couple it with lifelong patterning and our built-in ego response mechanism, it can be difficult to change!

When I was younger, someone told me that they had spent time in a monastery, and as they observed the monks, they marveled at how peaceful and centered the monks were as they went about their day. My response to this person was, "I am sure *I* could be peaceful and centered all the time, if I too was protected from the chaotic and demanding world around me!" I added, "I challenge one of those monks to walk in my shoes for one day, and let's see how he fares." It can be difficult to maintain your center and sense of peace when you're caught up in the tides of everyday life. Nobody is saying it isn't!

When someone tells me they are disappointed with their progress in their expansion of consciousness, I remind them how brave and courageous they are to even attempt this journey and that they need to be gentle with themselves. As we should not be judgmental of others on their human journey, nor should we stand in judgment of ourselves as we set upon our own. As it has been said, "Love your neighbor as yourself." This does not mean you have to *like* what your neighbor is doing or what you have done, but love him and yourself anyway, for in your loving, you are acknowledging the higher Self in him and in you. True love has no human conceptualization.

As I slowly awakened and became witness to my own insanity and the collective insanity of human consciousness, I was shocked by what I saw and terribly grief stricken. I also had the realization that even when I functioned at my highest level of human consciousness, that this level of consciousness was still was not enough, as I was still *of* the world. I was startled to become aware that when I thought I was demonstrating my higher Self, I really wasn't—it was only a very human sense of my spirituality. I readily became aware of the limitations inherent in functioning in an ego-based way as we muddle through life.

I often shook my head, as I had done so many times in my relationship with my sister, and said out loud, "What have I been thinking? What have I been doing? This is pure madness." And in that moment of awakening, my awareness of my transgressions was revealed to me.

As I progressed in my knowing, I became aware that there are not only human laws we live by, but laws that govern the higher consciousness of Self. In the human consciousness, there is a law that says, "Do unto others as you would have them do unto you." In the law of higher Self, or Soul consciousness, the corresponding law would be, "That which you do unto another, you do tenfold unto yourself." In the higher consciousness of Self, the act we inflict on another is not the sin, although it may be morally wrong. The greater transgression that occurred was that of our own Self-denial. If most people knew better, they would do better in any given moment. That they *do not* know better is because they have lost their way. They have been mesmerized by appearances.

As has been written, "Go and sin no more, for your sins are forgiven." Be aware of where your transgressions originate—it is the cause that manifests as an effect. If we are truly living soulfully, there is no way that we would or could hurt another. Plain and simple, our transgressions are no more than acts of Self-denial. In the human consciousness, if you do something to another, it warrants an eye-for-an-eye type of retaliation. In the realm of the Soul, that which is done to another ends up hurting the offender much more than it hurts the person it happened to. This is because the Self-denial of whom we really are is what hurts us the most.

The crucifixion of Jesus illustrates the concept of self-denial or "sin" and demonstrates that our chosen path must be straight and narrow as one shifts into Soul consciousness—or, as it is sometimes called, Christ consciousness. Then said Jesus unto his disciples, "If any man will come after me, let him deny himself (human consciousness), and take up his cross, and follow me." "For whosoever will save his life shall lose it: and whosoever will lose his life for my name sake shall find it. For what is a profit, if he shall gain the whole world, and lose his own soul? Or what shall a man give in exchange for his soul?"[6] The cross symbolizes our human limitation of thought. As the crucifixion is the dying of the human self, or giving up the perceived power of the whole personality. I believe it is our own Self-denial of our potentiality that creates our inner turmoil. If we have any awareness, or sense the potentiality of our human experience, we may be experiencing a house divided within Self. As stated by Jesus, "And if a kingdom be divided against itself, that kingdom cannot stand." "And if a house be divided against itself, that house cannot stand."[7] I personally believe, "It then becomes a conscious choice for us to choose the way of our Soul or Christ Consciousness as we desire to no longer feel divided.

Jesus's final walk through the streets of Jerusalem, with the cross he was made to carry, is symbolic of our own awareness and awakening of the insanity of the human consciousness. As Jesus carried the heavy cross through Jerusalem, he was tormented and ridiculed, and many of his followers turned their backs to him. Jesus could not help but experience extraordinary grief and sadness in what he was witnessing. Jesus prayed for forgiveness for those persecuting him, for they did not know what they were doing.

Jesus's journey on the path to his crucifixion is not unlike ours, as we awaken to our own insanity and feel burdened by that which surrounds us. His final walk illuminates the awakening of man's inhumanity to man. Jesus showed us his ability to look beyond the appearances of his experience—the torment and ridicule—and derive the strength to forgive those who caused him pain.

On the day of his crucifixion, Jesus knew that his salvation (and the salvation of everyone present) would be found through the denial of appearances and in the "knowing" that he had a choice in the way he handled the situation. Jesus prayed with the awareness that if his persecutors knew better, then they would have done better. He knew that his persecutors had fallen under the spell of human consciousness, which is primarily based in duality, fear, and lack. He understood that they had forgotten who they were and who they had always been— beings much greater than the ego-based self. As Jesus declared a higher vision and purpose beyond human consciousness, his experience shifted into a "knowing," and eventually a "Beingness." Jesus made a conscious choice to behold the Soul or Christ consciousness in all individuals, especially those who persecuted him. This was his ascension process.

As you know, we are not encouraged by society to be our greater Self, which extends beyond the world's definition of greatness. We are not told that our true and higher Self is seated within us. In fact, we are often driven into the world of appearances to identify our self. As our awakening continues and we are able to acknowledge the power of human consciousness over us, we too can make the shift in consciousness, as portrayed by Jesus. We can know and choose another way of being, as Jesus did on the way to his crucifixion.

Jesus had a choice in his experience. By all appearances the path of choice was straight and narrow, just as ours is in choosing "The Path to Knowing." When Jesus went to Jerusalem, he said to his disciples, "Behold, we go up to Jerusalem; and the Son of man shall be betrayed unto the chief priest and unto the scribes, and they shall condemn him to death…And shall deliver him to the Gentiles to mock, and to scourge, and to crucify him: and the third day he shall rise again."[8] Jesus knew what was to come, and from my perspective, even though this destiny was not of his choosing, he was able to acknowledge the situation *as it was*. He *surrendered* all beliefs or ideas he may have had about the situation. He *allowed* that which was being revealed to him. He *accepted* what was given to him to experience and trusted that which was greater than himself.

Jesus's experience of carrying the cross was his awakening to the insufficiency and insanity of the human consciousness; his death represented man's propensity, over time, to allow the illusions of human consciousness to be overcome and to effectively "die" within him. His resurrection symbolizes his ascension or evolution to his Soul or Christ consciousness, from which point he was able to behold the Christ in all and look beyond the appearances of man. It also speaks to the eternal nature of the Soul, for the physical body may be susceptible to death, but the essence driving it, the Soul, lives on.

Soul versus Spirit

At the time of death, or even as we approach death, at some point, the Soul withdraws from the body. It is only when our life signs cease, such as our heartbeat and breath, that our life force, or Spirit, is gone, and we are pronounced dead. I can hear you saying, "Wait a minute. Are you saying that my Soul is different than my Spirit?" Indeed, I am. *Spirit* is the life force that animates all things, without distinction.

The *Soul* is unique to each individual, and it lives on, eternally, as that individual essence. When the Soul leaves the body, the Spirit can remain, for a time. When the Spirit leaves the body, life ceases to be, and one's physical existence has ended.

"How do you know all this?" you may ask. "I was not aware of having a Soul *and* a Spirit. I thought they were the same thing!"

It was during the last 36 hours of my mother-in-law's life that I witnessed this Spirit-Soul differentiation. Approximately a day and a half prior to Roselyn's death, it became apparent that she was struggling in her death process. A friend and I decided to pray for her well-being, without attaching to the appearance of it. As my friend and I held hands across Roselyn's bed, we began to pray, and as we prayed we could sense a great release, or a feeling of peace. As we continued in prayer, I saw a medium-blue cloudy essence, Roselyn's soul, leave her body. It emerged through the soles of her feet, and funneled up through the bridge we had created over her body with our outstretched arms. I sensed that her soul had been struggling for a way out, and as we prayed for her, a channel presented itself, and conditions aligned to enable her soul to exit her body. I would like to clarify that even though Roselyn's soul had left her body, it was still tethered to her body until her physical life ceased. When my husband came home from work that night, he said that something in the house felt different, but he could not identify what had changed. I shared with him my experience with his mother, and right away, he knew he had sensed that her soul had gone. It was not until the next evening that her physical body stopped functioning, as her spirit, or life force, diminished.

In examining the story of Jesus's crucifixion and Roselyn's final hours, it becomes evident that the Soul is the constant as we proceed on our path in the evolution of consciousness. We are our Soul, today, tomorrow, and forever. As we become aware of our Soul and embrace it, we avail ourselves of stages within that consciousness, as well as states of other levels of consciousness. We are fortunate to exist in a time when we do not have to leave our physical body to become aware of our Soul. As we ascend in our conscious awareness of our Soul, thereby allowing it to shine through us, our life expands in glorious ways.

Awareness and Ascension

When Jesus was said to arise from the dead, not everyone could see his resurrection, because only those of a like consciousness were able to see it. It is similar to when people speak of a soul mate—someone that they feel a deep, passionate connection with, and they do not understand why they feel as they do. With a soul partner, either consciously or unconsciously, we can see beyond the appearance of the other person's personality to connect with their soul in a deep and profound way. As Jesus's followers connected with his soul consciousness, they were able to visibly witness his ascension process and his eternal form. *Ascension* occurs as we shift from a human consciousness to a soul consciousness.

One of the best illustrations of soul awareness I have witnessed occurred during my time as a hospice nurse. So often, soon after the death of a loved one, a family member might verbalize guilt for not having been nicer to or more understanding of her deceased family member while they were alive. In most instances, the guilt is unwarranted. What I tried to explain to the family member was that their perception of the loved one had changed at the time of death— that once someone dies, the human personality tends to fall away, and the soul then becomes the primary communication vehicle. And so, upon the death of a loved one, any communication that occurs is now of a soul-to-soul nature.

I explained that, unfortunately, as humans function primarily from the ego, we usually communicate in a personality-to-personality way, rather than soul to soul. Communicating in this way has many drawbacks and limitations, while soul-to-soul communication is a truly loving and extraordinarily selfless experience. I also told the family member that if her loved one were standing right here in front of her, she would most likely interact with the loved one as she did before they died—so, really, there was no need for feeling guilty. As humans, most of us have not yet learned how to communicate soul to soul; rather, we still connect via personality to personality. However, as humanity continues on the path of consciousness expansion, at some point in our evolution, our primary communication will become soul to soul. Again, it takes looking past the appearance of one's personality to make a soul connection with someone.

Several years ago, I had a very powerful experience with this phenomenon. I was directly communicating with someone's soul, while she had no conscious awareness of what was occurring. The oddest part was that her soul communication was *so contrary* to her ego-personality communication. While I was hearing words coming out of her mouth, I could also hear, or sense, her soul's communication simultaneously. Until I could figure out what was occurring, I thought I was going crazy! I seemed to be communicating with this person on two different levels, *at the same time.* Her soul was lovely and delightful in its communication, whereas her personality was incongruent with her soul. It took me some time, but I finally realized that I was witnessing the power of the human ego against the conscious awareness of soul.

Once I understood what was occurring, I saw very clearly that, unless we consciously invite our soul into our daily lives, we will never experience the magnificence of another part of ourselves as humans: our soul's capacity. I share this story to assure you that we all have a higher, more evolved aspect of ourselves just waiting to be invited into our lives. Once you decide to learn to live soulfully, your ego will most likely attempt to show you that your efforts are fruitless, because it is afraid of its own annihilation. Don't be discouraged— carry on in your pursuits.

Our soul mate, soul partner, or human soul connection experience is not unlike the experience of Jesus, for those that were able to see Jesus after his resurrection were able to experience a soul connection and communicate with him in a way that was foreign to most people. Those that were able to see Jesus resurrect from the dead witnessed the spectacle of eternal life, in which our personality falls away upon our physical death but our soul lives on forever. Just as Jesus had a soul connection with his followers, we also have soul connections with people in our lives. Jesus showed us that through a new awareness and an elevated level of consciousness, we too can look beyond appearances and rise and behold our Soul or Christ consciousness. As we hold a higher state of Being, we also attract the higher consciousness of others to us. As it is said, "Water reaches its own level." I believe that, as we have human families, we also have soul families.

Jesus was consumed with grief over the actions of those who turned against him, and yet, he showed us that the only path that transcends human appearances is one of a different vision. In the carrying of the cross, his resurrection, and his ascension, Jesus demonstrated for us the journey out of human consciousness into one that is based in the Soul. He showed us the possibility of not accepting human consciousness as our way of Being and demonstrated that, with continued awareness of choice, we too can live a life in which detachment, surrender, allowing, and acceptance reigns.

A more modern-day story that depicts the same theme is The Wizard of Oz.[9] By exploring the story of The Wizard of Oz, as with many other stories, if you look hard enough, you will find the same concepts as those related by the account of Jesus's crucifixion. I am sure most of you have seen the The Wizard of Oz movie, or have read the book, so let's look at concepts in this story that depict a similar journey of evolution in consciousness.

The story of The Wizard of Oz takes place in Kansas, where Dorothy lives with her aunt and uncle, and of course her dog Toto, when a tornado hits. The tornado illustrates the inner turmoil that Dorothy encountered as she embarked on her journey of her awakening of consciousness.

As Dorothy makes her way to Oz, she encounters good witches and bad witches, friends, dangers, and betrayals, just as we do in our own everyday lives. In this way, Dorothy awakened to and experienced the awareness of what the human level of consciousness holds for us. Her encounters along the yellow-brick road depict a world of ego-based, self-survival mentality (which hearkens back to Jesus' story). We, like Dorothy and Jesus, wonder at times why such insanity occurs. We ask, "What is lacking in us, and in those around us, and in society as a whole, to create such madness?" We constantly ask ourselves, "Why would a person *want* to inflict pain or suffering on another?"

Dorothy, Toto, and her friends—the Tin Man, the Lion, and the Scarecrow—all illustrate a part of us that we seek—courage, heart, and wisdom. However, like these characters, we think these attributes lie outside of us, so we seek it from others. When we don't get it from them, we are disappointed! We lash out at others, when we are, in reality, responsible for our own Self-denial. As the story goes, the characters follow the yellow brick road, and they quickly find that they must stay on the designated path and not be diverted by appearances of any sort. As they travel along the path, Dorothy makes everyone aware that her goal is to go back home—symbolically, her desire is to return to Self.

Dorothy is told that the Wizard who lives in the Emerald City should be able to help her get home, and the Tin Man, Scarecrow, and Lion decide to join her. Dorothy is constantly bombarded by images of the world, or human consciousness, which she no longer wants any part of. She chooses instead to stay on the straight and narrow path of the yellow-brick road.

Dorothy does get diverted off her path from time and time, but because she is so determined, she picks herself up, dusts herself off, and gets back on the path that leads to the Wizard. She encounters the good witch—symbolic of her soul, gently encouraging and guiding her to stay on track—and the bad witch, representative of her ego-self attempting to sabotage her journey home. Dorothy, not unlike Jesus, awakens to the human insanity and betrayal that surrounds her, and says at one point, "Why are you so mean?"

The Tin Man's desire for a heart, the Scarecrow's wish for a brain, and the Lion's longing for courage all indicate aspects of Dorothy that she must acknowledge before she can return home—to the home of

Self. Similarly, as Michelangelo skillfully tapped away at the stone to unveil the sculpture of David, Dorothy looks for aspects of herself to clarify on her journey to her higher Self. We observe the shift in Dorothy as she leaves Kansas and moves from a human-based consciousness to a soul-based awareness as she journeys to Oz.

Eventually, the group of friends reaches the Emerald City. At the doorway to the Emerald City, symbolizing the door to one's soul, they are told that the Wizard will not see them. Dorothy insists on seeing the Wizard and is eventually granted an audience with him. In this scenario, Dorothy is still seeking an outside power to guide and direct her in fulfilling her desire to return home. How many times in our own lives are we untrue to ourselves, seeking answers from sources that do not reside in our inner "knowing"? We often put our trust in sources outside of us, instead of listening to the wisdom of our higher Self.

Dorothy and her friends finally meet with the Wizard, who frightens them terribly; but because of their belief that their power resides outside of themselves, they plead with him for help. Eventually, they are told that their wishes will be granted. However, Toto tugs at the curtain that covers the godlike form of the Wizard, and when the curtain falls away, it reveals that the Wizard is nothing more than an ordinary man. The Wizard illustrates to us that we often give our power away to others who appear to be more powerful or more knowledgeable than we are. Too often, we think someone else knows better than we do what's right for us, rather than trusting our Self to guide us.

Toto pulling the curtain down is indicative of the collapse of the veil of human consciousness and shows the falsehood of our belief in powers outside of ourselves. After the Wizard is revealed, he informs Dorothy, the Tin Man, the Scarecrow, and the Lion that the qualities they were seeking were within them all along. The Wizard shows each character that through their acts of kindness, wisdom, or courage along the yellow-brick road, they demonstrated the very attributes they were seeking. The Wizard encouraged them to recognize what it took for them to reach the Emerald City—that the path was "straight and narrow" and that it took much determination. He acknowledged that even though appearances were scary at times, they were still able to look beyond them as they determined to reach the Emerald City.

As the Tin Man, Scarecrow, and Lion acknowledged and claimed the desired aspects of their consciousness, Dorothy was then free to go home. Dorothy learned that she could have gone home anytime—that all she had to do was click the heels of her ruby-red slippers. All it would have taken was for her to acknowledge her choice of a new operating system, or a higher state of consciousness. Dorothy's trials and tribulations would have been lessened and experienced differently had she simply deferred to her higher Self, which had been with her the whole time.

Like Dorothy, we all experience our own wicked witch (the ego) or the wicked witch of others as we travel our respective paths in search of home. The wicked witch kept trying to steal Dorothy's ruby slippers, because she intuitively knew the power within them—the power of our Souls. She feared annihilation if Dorothy discovered the truth.

I find the symbol of Dorothy's ruby slippers most interesting, for all she needed to do in any given moment was to click her heels together to return home. As we reclaim the power of our higher Self, all we need to do is make that click—our inner click—anytime we desire to return home. All it takes is a shift in consciousness, as we let go of what has been.

I have a coffee mug on my desk that says, "Dear Dorothy: Hate Oz, Took the shoes, Find your own way home! Toto."

Don't we all feel like Toto at times? We get so tired of wading around in our human experience (Oz), that we eventually decide we have had enough. We embark on our journey home, even though we may have to leave others behind. As I remind myself often, everyone's journey home is unique to them and occurs in the appropriate sequence and time that their soul has designed. If we look at others and think they are further ahead than us, we will lose. If we look at others and think *we* are further ahead than they are on their journey, we lose again. Our journey is our journey, and we need to honor that, and realize that it is unique to us. Remember that it is the journey that leads to the destination of our greater Self; and very few have made it to the destination without the journey. So enjoy the journey. "It is as it is."

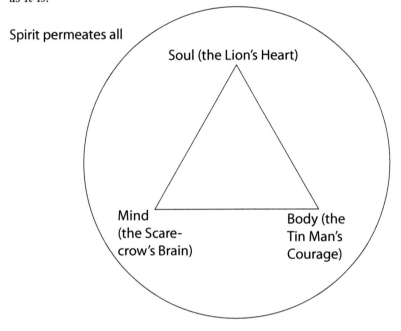

Spirit permeates all

Soul (the Lion's Heart)

Mind (the Scare-crow's Brain)

Body (the Tin Man's Courage)

This diagram illustrates the level of human consciousness, which leads us to the doorway of the Soul, or Christ consciousness. The triangle represents the emergence of transformation of our linear-based experience (our mental, emotional, physical, and spiritual way of functioning), to a mind-, body-, and Soul-based way of Being. The Soul, as it is positioned at the top of the triangle, is the higher aspect of ourselves that we are seeking, and when we choose it, our Soul becomes our primary way of being as we awaken to our greater knowing. By making the choice to walk differently in our world, our minds and bodies are now *expressions* of our Soul, and our life becomes much more than we could ever have envisioned. I would just like to note that even though our mind and body may express our Soul, it is still very important to nurture and care for our personal sense of self, for without these human aspects we would not have an avenue of expression.

What we call our higher Self really does not matter. You may prefer to use different terminology—but no matter what words you use, the theme is the same. As it is said, there are many rooms in a mansion, and many doors to each room; yet they all exist within the same mansion. What I am offering to you is the doorway I have discovered. If it makes sense to you, that is fine, and if it does not make sense to you, that is also fine. No matter what you take away from this book, I hope it encourages you to seek your own individualized truth.

Like Jesus and Dorothy, I too understand that the journey can be difficult at times. I proceed with the conviction of my own ascension—owning that which I am. When we finally awaken, there is no way back. Life will continue to offer the experiences you need to reconnect with your true Self, revealing to you, one day at a time, the world of inner guidance you have available to you. As I evolve and grow in consciousness, I am committed to allowing my false perceptions to die away daily. I do this by *acknowledging* that "It is as it is" and by *surrendering* not only to the situation at hand, but to the greater knowing of that which lies within me, in the depths of my soul. I *allow* my mental activity to stand behind me, and I walk forward, without attachment, and say or do what is revealed to me from within. I then *accept* that which presents itself in my outer world, because I know that it has come forth from my higher Self.

This process, which I strive to live on a daily basis, is not without its moments of projecting my power elsewhere and then awakening to and witnessing my folly. However, I make the choice every day to stand firm and allow my own ascension to be revealed to me.

7

The Still, Small Voice

When you embark on the journey back to your soul, the lessons and opportunities you need along the way keep coming to help you grow into who you really are. For me, the lessons came as a flood (literally!). My mother's home is situated by a lake, and, during the fall, heavy rains caused the water level of the lake to rise dramatically. Faced with the likelihood of a flood, I had two choices: I could panic, or I could choose for the experience to be more soulful in nature.

I went through the steps of "The Path to Knowing," which I outlined earlier. I took a moment to quiet myself and listen to the still, small voice within, but I did not hear any particular guidance, so I set about the things that needed to be done. First I secured anything outside the home that could potentially float away. I raised my mother's motorboat to the highest level possible, and tied it to the lift cradle with rope. Then I decided to take her Jet Ski out of the water, because it was beginning to float out of its cradle. However, I needed someone to help me. Just as I made this decision, a neighbor came wading out through the water in the street and asked me if I needed any help. He agreed to help me with the Jet Ski. With the boat and the Jet Ski secured, I surveyed the situation and gauged the possibility of water reaching the house. I decided to wait and see what would happen.

As the days progressed, several homes across the street were surrounded by water. The street had completely flooded, with the water slowly inching up the driveway of my mother's home. The neighbors on my side of the street had begun placing sandbags around their homes, and I felt that I needed to decide on a strategy. When I took a moment to listen to that still voice within me, I received a clear message that the home would survive the flood, and I need not do anything more. However, I have to admit that the appearance that surrounded me triggered another story, which was one of fear and uncertainty. I felt responsible for my mother's home, and if I made the wrong choice, I would feel badly if her home suffered water damage. There was a lot at stake, and I needed to make the correct decision as to how to proceed. I wavered in my conviction of my inner knowing, as I literally waded through the world of appearances.

By now, the water had risen way beyond the seawall, and there were no signs to indicate that the flooding would recede anytime soon. The township was offering to bring in sandbags for homeowners to protect their homes from the flooding, and I had to decide whether to take action while the support was available. I went back and forth, and as a battle ensued within me, I questioned if I should sandbag or stand firm in my knowing. In the end, I was swayed by appearances, so I started to place sandbags at the most vulnerable areas of the house. I laid 750 sandbags, all by myself, within a 2-day period of time. As the water kept rising, I would either add height to my sandbag wall, or extend the wall as warranted. When all was said and done, the lake water had risen 5 feet and came within 1 foot of my mother's home foundation and garage door. Over the next week, the water receded.

Afterward, I examined my experience and thought about the many hours I had spent laying sandbags unnecessarily. I surmised that it was just another opportunity for me to feel secure in living what I believe. I had to ask myself, Why did my experience turn out the way it did? What more did I need to learn? I realized that, if I had only had the courage and conviction to listen to my inner voice, I would have saved myself a lot of back-breaking work—let alone having to remove all the sandbags once the water had gone back to its usual level! I did acknowledge that, even though I did not listen to my higher Self, things did progress in an orderly fashion, as evidenced by the neighbor who appeared to help me take the Jet Ski out of the water, and by the fact that, when I chose to sandbag, the bags were delivered to me. The most important thing I took away from this experience was that I had only functioned from my human consciousness, and not from my soul. In the end, I was very grateful for the way it all turned out. I had learned that there was another way for me to be proactive in this experience, which I was not able to embrace because of my overwhelming fear.

I realized that what I needed to examine for myself was twofold: How do I differentiate my inner voice from my mind chatter? And once I've accomplished that, how do I allow my inner voice to be the one that I listen to? I concluded that, through continued practice in trusting in my higher knowing in experiences of lesser consequence, I would gain strength in my conviction when faced with more important situations. What I *will* say about my experience with the lake flooding is that, even though I was not able to accept my inner knowing, things still unfolded in a more blessed way than they might have if I had panicked and not checked in with my inner Self to begin with.

I realized that my knowing might come in the moment, or it might even come later. I have found that the still, small voice within, is just that—a very still, small voice—and that if the mind is rambling on in a chaotic manner, you will never be able to hear it. I also realized that my higher knowing may come as an "inner click," indicating that a connection with my Self has been made, or it might come as an inner sense of knowing that all is well. The still, small voice is experiential (without thought or intellect) rather than active and engaging—and it occurs while making that inner connection in silence. The silence comes if you can disengage from any thinking, emotionality, or reactivity; it is purely the experience of Being; and in our essence of Being, our connection is made. Have you ever had an experience when you were able to observe your reaction or response in a particular situation, only to inwardly witness that your ego was functioning, not your higher Self? I have, and as I have watched this aspect of myself, I had to laugh at the childish behavior I was witnessing as I wanted to be heard or right. Be aware that the ego self is loud and boastful and with attachment, while the higher Self, as a knowing, is very matter-of-fact and without attachment.

After my experience at the lake, I again committed to choosing the way I wanted to walk in the world, in every way that I could. Have you ever encountered this coincidence—that, just when you think you are living a concept that you want to embody, you suddenly get another learning opportunity to test your progress?

Well, my opportunity came as a tugging on my heartstrings. Out of the blue, my husband and I were asked to adopt a young child. Immediately, I withdrew to engage my higher Self in search of guidance. I knew this was a situation not to be taken lightly or to be decided hastily. I did wonder about the timing of this request, because within a week, we were taking our son to college, which would leave us with one empty bed in our home.

Since no strong inner guidance came forth, I decided to set about what I felt to be necessary in this situation. My husband and I discussed all the pros and cons of adopting a young child, and we explored the legal aspects of adoption. We discussed with our children the prospect of adopting the child, for we valued their thoughts and opinions. My husband and children were strongly for the adoption. For myself, however, I had not heard that still voice within giving me guidance—so I delayed making any decision.

From a human perspective, I rationalized that I had already raised two other children besides my own, so how difficult could it really be to raise another child? I firmly believe that, as adults, we have a responsibility to all children to protect them and to be their advocates. I had to ask myself, "Why was I not willing to live this belief?" I continued to await my inner guidance, but it did not come. As the last one holding out in my family, I was being pressured, and was assured by all concerned that they would be supportive in every way. I even had several friends offer to volunteer to babysit, if needed.

I was extremely torn. What was the appropriate decision? I wanted my soul's perspective, a nod from my higher Self—but no knowing or guidance come forth—and I mean, *none.* It was only when it came down to the wire, when we had to commit and make the legal decision to adopt, that the still voice from within me spoke up—and I sensed, very clearly, that I should not adopt the child. I was surprised. I thought, How could my greater Self *not* want to care for this innocent child, who is surrounded by such chaos? I pondered, Why was my inner knowing so incongruent with my human convictions as a responsible adult? As I reflected on this knowing, my mind wandered to my recent experience at the lake.

I rekindled the experience of surrendering and allowing my higher Self to direct me in that situation, only to deny my knowing in the end. I sandbagged when I knew without a doubt that everything would turn out fine if I did not sandbag. In that situation, however, I was unable to get beyond the immediate appearances. Ultimately, I gave in to the fear of what I was told or thought might happen if I did not sandbag. My fear overrode my knowing that everything would be fine. So my decision to sandbag was purely fearful and ego based.

In my present adoption predicament, I decided that not listening to my higher Self would create more pain in the long run than the pain of not doing what I believed a responsible adult should do in my shoes. This time, I stood firm in my knowing, for I knew, without a doubt, that I had received an impartation from my soul. I also knew that it would not be in the best interest for all of us to disallow and not accept that knowing. I felt the "knowing" so deeply, in fact, that I never will forget it. Unlike my experience with the lake, this time, the knowing felt like having a very clear sense of what to do, rather than hearing a small voice.

Needless to say, my decision was unpopular, and I received much negative feedback from my children and others. I felt tormented. My ego waged an inner battle, questioning my knowing and causing me a great amount of grief. From a very human, ego-based perspective, I could not understand why my inner guidance would direct me not to adopt. I also disagreed with my soul, because I could not believe that such an honest desire to care for a child could not be for the highest good. Eventually I had to surrender, however, and as I moved further away from the situation, I was able to allow it to be as it should be. If it was meant to be different, it would have been. What I realized was that sometimes our inner guidance may not make sense, as it hadn't made sense to me—but we must continue to trust in it, no matter what.

Twice, after making a final decision to not adopt, we were again approached by different individuals, who asked us to reconsider adopting this child. Each time I was approached, I followed the process, the "Path to Knowing," and each time, I received the same answer as before. While it's not a rationalization, as I step back and observe the situation from a much higher place, I understand a little better why I received the message as I did. As of this moment, I stand firm in the conviction of the knowing I received in the silence. I will continue to believe it until I receive different guidance. Once I was able to relinquish myself from the adoption situation, other avenues began to unfold for the child, and he is doing well.

What I would like to convey through this story is that our inner guidance may not appear appropriate at face value, according to our human standards. The challenge becomes the continuation of believing in our higher conviction, until directed otherwise. I truly believe that our higher Self can consider all potential possibilities and express the best for all concerned. It can express our highest good, and the highest good for everyone involved, in a much better way than that of our humanness. It takes the fortitude of surrendering and allowing to birth possibilities or awareness beyond that of limited human functioning. I am also acutely aware that the still, small voice can easily be overpowered or negated by the ego; and when push comes to shove, the ego will win, unless we learn to stand in the knowing of our Soul. It is important to remember that the still, small voice not only has access to multiple possibilities, but that it considers our level of consciousness and the things we need to learn as we evolve.

Another very interesting observation I acquired from my brush with adoption is that at different states of consciousness (or stages in consciousness), we can be a healer or a mystic. A healer, by definition, might attempt to fix an ailment or problem while standing in a higher state of consciousness, whereas a mystic stands in a state of nonattachment to the situation and is not swayed by appearances. The mystic steps into the Presence of the All Knowing in the moment and allows a greater understanding to unfold.

What I have found on my path is that the initial level of my detachment tends to predict how quickly I am able to receive inner guidance, direction, or inner peace. When it comes to living a soulful life, I have found that it comes in waves, or bits and pieces, and that it involves a conscious effort on a daily basis. However, I have to say that the periods of my greater awareness or "knowing" are becoming more frequent. More and more, I am able to live my human life from a place of Soul or Christ consciousness. As one resides in Soul consciousness, it eventually evolves into a "Beingness," with an indescribable quietness deep inside that feels almost surreal.

8

The Eye of the Needle

As humans having an earthly experience, we have two distinct levels of consciousness available to us as our primary operating system: a human-based consciousness or a soul-based consciousness. Most of us default to a human-based consciousness. Our new way of Being begins with a personal reflection of one's life and the awareness of ownership of one's emotions and reactivity toward others or toward situations. This first step takes courage and a commitment to self-responsibility. It also requires a desire to no longer exhibit or claim a victim mentality.

In the initial steps of our evolution, it is not uncommon for our ego to attempt to sabotage our efforts or for those around us to not affirm our new way of operating in life. We must be aware that people in our lives have learned to respond to us the way that we have always been, and now, suddenly, we are asking them to play by another set of rules, when they are not even aware of a game change. This sudden change in our behavior can initially create much internal and external stress, if others are not accepting of the new you. As I continue to evolve in consciousness, I say to myself, "I am that which I seek," as I affirm my ongoing desire to grow in consciousness.

As human beings, we tend to dislike change, let alone sudden change; so our change may appear to come slowly, as we practice. It is like starting a new diet and taking responsibility for your health, only to have someone tempt you with a piece of chocolate cake. Do you stand firm in your desire to claim health for yourself, or do you allow your ego to sabotage you by rationalizing the desire to eat the cake? As I have said, there is always a choice of a new operating system available to us.

You may find that, as you evolve in consciousness, people in your life may tend to come and go, or even fall away. Do not be surprised if, initially, when you awaken to the insanity in your personal world and the world in general, you experience grief and sadness. It is a sadness of such depth that, unless you have experienced it, you might not understand. As I began to observe the insanity in my life and the world in a new way, I experienced immense grief for a period of time. However, along with the grief came a "mountaintop view" of my life.

As I looked down at the circumstances of my life, I had this unusual insight: Even though I had believed I was living my heart's desire of a spiritual existence, it still was not enough in this world of insanity. I realized that my spiritual path was, in many ways, a higher-level functioning of my human consciousness and was still based outside of myself. I now understood that I had been no more than a human being having a spiritual experience, rather than a soul having a human experience. I realized that my soul connection was hit or miss, and that it really had not been my predominant experience, even though I thought I had evolved so far on my journey.

As we continue to evolve in consciousness, we become aware that there is a longing for something in our lives that we just cannot seem to grasp or put words to. We may feel like something is missing, even though all of our earthly desires have been met. We may think that if we find just the right spiritual guru or attend another lecture, it will help us discover what we are missing.

A spiritual mentor, a special guru, a new book, or a lecture may be important at some point in our journey, but these things are still outside of ourselves. They can only help us get *to* the doorway or maybe even *through* the doorway to the soul—*but no one other than ourselves can get us through the eye of the needle.* We may realize that such practices as positive thinking, affirmation, and prayer can help to elevate us to another state or level of consciousness of receptivity—but the effectiveness of these practices stops at some point. It is only upon the experiential passing through the eye of the needle that we are no longer separate from Self. It is our separateness from Self that causes us pain, suffering, and fear. I invite you to read "The Soulful Living Agreement" at the end of this book. After you insert your name, witness it for yourself or have someone witness your claim of adopting a new operating system in your life. With this agreement, you are making a conscious choice of the way you want to walk in your life. You have made the choice to be the "captain of your own ship," and within that choice, you opt for soulful living.

The process that I have identified does not deny the ego; rather, it allows us to initially sidestep the ego in an intentional way. Then, as you progress in your practice, you can invite your ego to participate in a new way—as a support, not a driving force. What I have experienced over time, as I have become more aware of and comfortable with my soul presence, is that my mental, emotional, physical, and spiritual functioning has transformed and transcended to a mind-and-body capacity that expresses my Soul.

When we become aware of our Soul presence, we know we have embarked on a journey of Soul consciousness or Christ consciousness. After we have made this realization, there is no more intellectualizing. The experience is like threading a needle—you cannot go *around* the eye of the needle to thread the needle; you have to stand steadfast and go through the center, or the eye, of the needle. Passing a piece of thread through the tiny eye of the needle may appear difficult and impossible at times, but with focus and determination, it can be done.

As we pass through our own "eye of the needle" to commune with our greater Self, it can be done through the doorway of *acknowledging,* "It is as it is," *surrendering, allowing,* and *accepting.* Then, as we pass through the eye, our "knowing" occurs in a state of receptive silence, with little space for error. It is in this receptivity of silence that our true Self or this higher state of consciousness is experienced. If one tries to put a large piece of thread through the eye of the needle, it will not pass—similarly, in our passage, if we try to go through the eye while carrying any baggage of personality, fear, or ego, we will not be able to make it. As we pass through the eye of the needle, our Soul has the opportunity to express through us at this level of consciousness at our current stage of evolution.

The Doorway to Knowing initially acknowledges our Soul; we become familiar with our Soul—we intellectualize about our Soul. By passing through the eye of the needle, we experience Oneness with our Soul, and have now opened to our greater potentiality as Soul having a human experience. We have allowed and accepted our higher Self to be available to us; and as we recognize our Soul, we also allow an even a greater consciousness to be available to us if we desire it.

As we evolve to our state of higher Self, it is done without taking thought with us, and as we eventually become One with our higher Self, this stage of experience becomes a "Beingness" with All That Is and has ever been. Through our expansion of consciousness, we experience Oneness with all as our life is now fluid without effort. We are able to understand the "circle of life" in a new and unique way. We are that which we seek, as we realize we have always been that which we have sought.

As I touched on earlier, the way is straight and narrow and not without its moments of wanting to throw in the towel. It is not a journey for the meek or mild, and it takes constant self-evaluation and self-discipline to not only pass through the doorway to enlightenment but to also pass through the eye of the needle to live Soulfully in our "Beingness." Once we have reclaimed our Soul, which can bring forth our higher knowing, we begin another journey into our potential as

Souls living Soulfully. I describe living Soulfully as an inner quietness, or a sense of "nothingness," which is beyond all understanding.

My path has shown me that I can live Soulfully in one moment and revert to my old ways in another moment. And so, as I have said all along, every moment becomes a choice and an opportunity to practice that which is available to us in this human experience.

As we evolve in Soul or Christ consciousness, we explore the many stages that reside within it. As we do so, we experience periods of enlightenment that further aid us in our ascension. Ultimately, it is in the silence that we await and allow our higher Self to come forth.

The experience of Soul or Christ consciousness has nothing to do with mental activity. As we become aware of the possibilities birthed by our recognition of our soul capacity, it is now our mind and body that express our enlightenment in our human or third-dimensional life. To *not* invite our mind and body to be an active part in our Soul experience would leave us empty as human beings, and there would be no purpose in having this earthly experience.

Our ascension to enlightenment is energetic and vibratory in nature. It is accessible to us through our Soul capacity and is converted into a form that the mind or body can translate and understand. And so, the Soul is the capacity to access our higher states and stages of consciousness that we are already and to allow our enlightenment or awareness to become our human experience.

About 10 years ago, while vacationing, I was faced with a medical predicament. It was similar to one I had encountered several years prior, which necessitated surgery. When I first realized the significance of what I was experiencing, I decided very firmly that I was not going through what I had before, and that I knew without a doubt there was more to it than just the appearance of the situation. There had to be another way.

After my husband and I put the children to bed one night, I asked him to pray with me. I was in so much physical pain and discomfort that my husband read to me from one of the metaphysical books I was reading at the time. My husband stayed awake with me for most of the night, and we prayed nonstop. It was probably around 4 o'clock in the morning, when my husband had fallen asleep, that I began to pray by myself in earnest. I did not pray to God to heal me, but I prayed to be an empty vessel for the expression of the principle that I am One with the Intelligence That Knows and Is All. I reminded myself that, even before I ask, I have always been enveloped in the power and presence of the greatness of All. I repeated with feeling and knowing that "I Am That I Am." I asserted that I am One in consciousness with All That Is, and that I am victorious in my knowing. I maintained this as my principle of focus. I did not ask for healing—I just remembered, in every moment, my true nature. I had to let the fear and pain be "what they were," without attaching to them in any way, and allow my higher Self to be present.

My prayers helped me stay focused, or straight and narrow in my thinking, which eventually brought me to and through the doorway of my soul. As I became One with my soul, I sat in receptive silence, and in the blink of an eye, I passed through the eye of the needle—for my experience was no longer a *knowing,* but an *allowing.* I was still awake, and as my eyes drifted to the corner of the room, I saw a bright, ruby-red light swirling in a spiral motion, and in that moment I knew I had made contact with the "I Am That I Am." I felt an overwhelming sense of peace, and then I fell asleep. When I awoke several hours later, the pain and discomfort had subsided by ninety percent, and I knew that, with time, all discomfort would be gone. I knew without a doubt that I had experienced what could be called a miracle, or an instantaneous healing; however, the miracle was not of an external appearance, as one might think. *The miracle I had experienced was my conscious remembrance of who I am, in this greater consciousness of creation.*

The miracle was the recognition of the principle, "I Am That I Am," and nothing more. The miracle was my conviction to not be swayed by appearances and to never question my knowing or enlightenment. Can you imagine what might have happened if, after my making my Soul connection, I focused on the residual pain rather than the miracle? I predict that the miracle or knowing would have been negated in time. It is similar to a miracle of regaining sight after a lifetime of blindness. As you revel in your newfound sight, a loved one comes to you and asks you if you are still blind. Suddenly, you recall the memory of not being able to see—and with that, you cannot see again.

What happens after the occurrence of many miracles is that we just cannot let go of what was, to allow what *is* in our greater knowing. The mind always wants to track back to what has been, rather than being in the moment; and within this mental activity, we have lost the momentum of our knowing. The miracle in any healing, be it physical or otherwise, is our inner connection with our higher Self and All That Is, as we look beyond appearances. The miracle is our conscious remembrance of the true nature of our Being, the "I Am That I Am."

With regard to my healing experience, I want you to know that I did follow up with my physician the next day, who decided that there was nothing to do but wait and see if I continued to feel well—which I did. The healing I experienced was singular, as I have not had an experience that dramatic since. Do not be misled by my experience, for I share it with you to illustrate what is possible in our humanness— yet caution is necessary when it comes to the consistency of such a dramatic occurrence at our, or at least my, present level of evolution. As discussed, our outer world or experience tends to be a reflection of our inner world or level of consciousness. If we are having a particular experience, it is because it lies in the realm of our consciousness, and it is appearing *as it is* for some reason. If you find me injured and bleeding, or if you come upon someone having a heart attack, call 911 by all means, and *then* implement the "Path to Knowing." Implementing the "Path to Knowing" will help shift the situation to a higher level of awareness and consciousness and allow a greater knowing to unfold in the experience, as we engage in the situation.

I would like to share one more healing experience. This time, my healing did not take the form that I would have imagined, because— unbeknownst to me at the time—I was attached to a different outcome.

Since my early childhood, I have believed from the depth of my soul in our potentiality as humans, which includes spontaneous healing experiences, among other extraordinary possibilities. As I have learned during my life, seeing or believing does not necessarily mean we can live the wisdom of whatever has been revealed to us. Because we have the ability to draw from the next state or stage of consciousness, it does not mean we are able to consistently demonstrate it in our lives just yet. As I experienced, sometimes the ego can get ahead of us with respect to living what we know to be true and possible.

So when I noticed that a small red spot had appeared on the tip of my nose, I brushed it off as "nothing." As the spot began to grow and change, I concluded that it would be healed within its own time, and I did nothing. When the spot continued to grow, I implemented the "Path to Knowing." However, I did not listen to my higher Self or my knowing, because my higher Self told me that I should undergo a biopsy, and this was exceedingly hard for me to accept. Instead, I held to my ego-based belief, which insisted that it *could* and *would* go away on its own. The fact that I could come away with a scar on the tip of my nose only reinforced my ego-self stance to do nothing.

Similar to the story of the man who drowned and then asked God why he did not save him, I did not listen or acknowledge my inner guidance, nor did I concede that our good comes from many avenues. On two occasions, I had an opportunity to undergo a biopsy, which I declined both times. It was only after a friend of mine, whom I normally do not see very often, said something to me about the spot on my nose, that I was awakened from the illusion of "wellness" created by my ego. Upon my awakening to my present circumstance, I scheduled a biopsy. The spot on my nose *did* need to be surgically removed, and its removal did create a scar (though thankfully not a horrible one). And so, my original fear of having a scar in such a visible place became a reality. And yet, I walked away from the experience having learned a most valuable lesson.

I consider myself to have experienced a healing, though not a physical one, as my ego would have liked. Rather, I have experienced a healing of my ego. Again, I have been presented with yet another opportunity to consciously awaken and become more familiar with my higher Self, as I lessen my ego-driven, everyday guide. It also reaffirmed for me that looking beyond appearances does not negate what is before us in the physical realm. Rather, a recognition of the physical manifestation ("It is as it is") can be used to shift us out of the consciousness that created the experience in the first place, if we so choose. As we shift out of our present state of consciousness, we avail ourselves of our higher Knowing in any situation, in whatever way it presents itself. It is important to note that we do not always need to be cognizant of the consciousness that created the situation, as we can still shift to another level of consciousness in any given moment. However, we do need to decide to be proactive, rather than reactive, if we are aware that an experience feels "off" or that it is making us feel uncomfortable.

As we become more open and receptive to our higher Self, that which we need to know as we evolve in consciousness will be revealed to us at the appropriate time. If we need to reevaluate or revisit some aspect of ourselves as we grow in consciousness, we will do so in a more gentle and productive way. Now that we are on a journey of being a willing participant in our lives, we will be consistently more aware of aspects of ourselves that hinder us or move us forward. As I was able to reaffirm and recognize that my situation *is as it is*, I finally surrendered, allowed, and accepted as I moved forward, being guided and directed by my higher Self in the resolution of the experience.

9

True Gratitude

I don't know about you, but from childhood through adulthood, I was instructed to give thanks or show gratitude for everything I had. When you think about it, we tend to be encouraged to give thanks for appearances and material objects in our lives, such as food, clothing, a home, a new car, good health, or a job. Too often, we neglect to show gratitude for that which preceded its appearance.

I have been traveling along the path of my awakening and enlightenment for as long as I can remember, and, fortunately for me, I met my first spiritual mentor at the age of sixteen. My mentor introduced me to different religions and philosophies and also assisted me in learning and exploring many consciousness-expanding techniques. Some of these techniques were positive thinking, visualization, meditation, affirmations, and prayer; and over time, I became skilled. I believed that these techniques were the cause of the effects that presented in my reality.

I knew that my affirmations could produce some manifestation; I knew that my positive thinking could redirect my outer experience in a powerful way. Through meditation, I could have spiritual experiences; through visualization, I could create a new reality. In some respects, I learned to appreciate the effects, or the reality, that stemmed from the cause.

As I have evolved in consciousness, I have become familiar with my higher Self, which is accessible from my Soul capacity. I hold much gratitude for my continued awakening on my journey of Self. In my seeking of another level of consciousness, I give gratitude for that which I seek, "I Am That I Am." I seek to know that which is greater than me, which I am. I explain this search to myself as, "I want to learn to fish." I want to live and have my Being in the I Am That I Am; I want to know and experience the potential of Oneness. Jesus fed the multitudes with a surplus of bread and fish on several occasions during his ministry, and he grew frustrated when no one wanted to learn the way to create the experience of the surplus for himself. Basically, no one wanted to experience their own ascension of consciousness; they did not want to be self-reliant or self-directed. Jesus's followers did not realize that all things would be given to them, if only they would do as Jesus taught.

As the Chinese proverb goes, Give a man a fish, and you feed him for a day. Teach a man to fish, and you feed him for a lifetime. In earnest, I want to be fed during my lifetime by that which is greater than me, yet *is* me at the same time.

My search began by trying to understand the nature of Infinite Intelligence, Source, or God. I wanted to become aware of Source and eventually to experience Source in a personal way. I had always heard the words, "I Am That I Am," and no matter how hard I tried, I could not fully understand this concept. I could never quite personalize this statement or principle.

As you might be aware, quantum science has arisen in the search for this unknown, unquantifiable presence that appears to function on the basis of a principle unlike the principles of human consciousness. In human consciousness, one might say that my thought is the cause of my reality. It manifests as an effect or a material reality. Additionally, in human consciousness, man has derived a series of laws that we collectively agree with and to which we abide, such as safety laws, religious laws (the Ten Commandments, for example), and unspoken ethical and moral laws.

In our Soul consciousness, we have transcended our human consciousness to a place of higher knowing or higher Self—and even at this stage of consciousness, there are still some limitations. The law in this stage of higher Self is that our denial of Self is the greatest transgression that we can experience. Not allowing the potentiality of our Soul to demonstrate itself in our lives leaves us feeling empty and powerless.

Here is the way I envision our journey to Soul consciousness. As we begin our human experience, we may start out on the bottom floor of a 20-story building, or we may even incarnate on a higher floor. As we decide to venture upward or evolve in consciousness, we climb to higher floors. As we ascend, we obtain a greater view or vantage point from which to see the surroundings of the building, or, in our case, our life experiences. This allows us to look at our lives from a whole new perspective.

As we continue to climb, we have awakenings and experiences that urge us to want to seek an even greater understanding of our existence or purpose. If we take a moment during our ascension to look out at everything that lies below, in that moment, we realize that everything "Is as it is"—that we are where we should be, having the experiences that we should be having, at our present state or stage of consciousness. Our experience cannot be any different than what it is. We are standing on the floor we ascended to, because we are! In that moment, we stop and offer gratitude for our state of consciousness or its representation in our world.

As we continue to ascend, we stand in awe of our awareness and potential as humans having this earthly experience. We continue to have experiences that help us evolve in consciousness, and as we climb each step, we become stronger and more determined to reach the top. We may climb to the floor on which our soul resides and say, "Wow, what a view!" We might even say, "I have come as far as I desire, and I am satisfied with the view," or we may continue climbing.

Usually, the gratitude we offer tends to be congruent with our current state or stage of consciousness. As we evolve, our gratitude shifts from the gratitude of effects, to gratitude for the cause. Our gratitude for the cause takes on a new essence in relation to our awareness, or reference point, as our consciousness level evolves.

As we become aware of our Soul presence on our climb or ascension in this state of consciousness, we can eventually allow or connect with the Infinite Intelligence, Source, or God, from our elevated Soul capacity. The law of this stage of consciousness shifts again in a new way. Our cause is now a nontangible, unquantifiable intelligence that Is All and Knows All; and through the access of our Soul, it comes forth into the world as form. The Soul, not unlike our mind and body, now allows and expresses the Infinite, the All-Knowing. This unquantifiable Presence is everything and seems to be light-based, whereas the soul appears as vibratory.

As I said before, scientists are searching for that which we are seeking, but I'm not sure they will ever be able to quantify its presence through scientific measurement. Science will never be able to emphatically identify Source, because its origin arises from a state of nothingness, to be transformed through awareness to express through us as a something. Source finds its expression through the beauty of the trees, the milky white clouds, our furry companions, and through us. So, at the level of Universal Consciousness, our gratitude is expressed for our Oneness with All—for Source, which expresses *through us (Soul Consciousness)* as its creation. As we are more aware and expand in consciousness, we can draw from the next state or stage of consciousness that is available to us as we evolve. Have you ever observed yourself as you stand in the muck of human consciousness to only later experience a profound moment? This is because as we experience consciousness, we can draw from the next state or stage of consciousness, yet we may default to the previous level at any time. As we make the choice to partake and experience the expansion of consciousness, we become aware of its fluidity as it ebbs and flows.

Our relationship with Source is Oneness, in its purest, most loving form; it is a reciprocal relationship of co-creator and creator—"I Am That I Am." "I Am I"—I am the co-creator, and the creator is in me. I Am Consciousness, and I Am Victorious, in my knowing and in my expression of it.

As we ascend or evolve from a creator in our small universe to a co-creator in the vast universe, our cause shifts from Self to Source. As we evolve in consciousness, our effects also shift, from a demonstration of our awareness available through our limited Self, to our awareness of our vast Self as One.

Our potential, in our expansion of consciousness, is to experience a true emergence with Source as Oneness. The cause and effect in life, at this level of consciousness, collapse upon themselves, and the Source cause and Source effect now become one as our Beingness. At this point in the evolution of consciousness, there is no separation between us and Source. There is no separation between us and our fellow man, for our connection is Oneness of Soul. At this level of consciousness, there is no need for human laws or religious or moral laws, for this is a relationship based on true love. Within this relationship, no harm could ever beset you. We become aware that the purpose of this human journey through our third-dimensional reality is to witness the cosmic expansion of consciousness as we experience its states and stages unfolding *as us*. It is all about disallowing the illusionary division that has created our blockage of Self.

I believe that *true* gratitude is giving thanks for the consistent, unwavering *principle* that creates or expresses its gifts in our lives. I give gratitude for the Infinite Intelligence, Source, or God presence and power that permeates me as an expression of my Oneness with All. I stand firm in my awareness on my path to knowing. "It is as it is." I surrender, allow, and accept that which is greater than me, as me, in my human expression. I offer much gratitude for "I am that which I seek," and for this magnificence expressing through me as I have this earthly experience. As we give consistent and honest gratitude, our convictions grow stronger, and we become that which we have been in search of since our birth.

I also hold much gratitude for my Soul presence, which has never abandoned me. Since my early childhood, I have never felt alone; and I give thanks for this Presence that has enveloped me, as I have always been guided, protected, and directed. While having this human experience, I give true gratitude for the opportunity to remember and explore the "I Am That I Am."

Acknowledgments

To my mother, Catherine (Kay), thank you for the encouragement and freedom to explore my own truth from a very young age, even when it made no sense. I have always appreciated you championing my explorative endeavors, while in pursuit of my higher Self.

To my husband and life partner, Jeff, I want you to know that without your love and support, this book could not have come to fruition. I thank you for the time I was given to cocoon and percolate, and for the freedom to be me. I am so grateful that we are together!

To my children, Matthew and Lauren, you have kept me humble, in a very loving way, while teaching me so much about myself and about life.

To my many mentors and teachers who have gently guided, directed, and prodded me at times along on my voyage of Self, Namaste!

To all my other family members, and friends—who are my family—thank you for walking this path with me. At times, it has been a wild ride.

And to those reading this book, I thank you for "Being" all that you are, and for the courage it takes to set about your journey in the evolution and expansion of consciousness. It is a noble one. As we each awaken to our full potentiality as human beings, the world cannot help but be a better place.

The Diagrammatic Journey to Self
The Evolution/Expansion of Consciousness

At birth or incarnation, we experience collective human consciousness and manmade laws. We overcome our basic human-survival needs as we climb up Maslow's pyramid of the hierarchy of needs, which is in no way a straight climb. We accumulate material things, and if we are not careful, they become our false footholds. If we experience a catastrophe or challenge, we may try to identify more with our spiritual or religious practice, or begin a new search for our spirituality. If we allow it, the journey in search of our true Self begins or continues, depending on our desire.

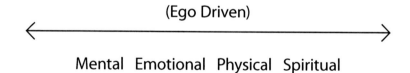

(Ego Driven)

Mental Emotional Physical Spiritual

As we begin our search for Self, our journey usually begins with an external focus, involving minimal self-reflection. However, as we are willing to take self-responsibility, we can shift to a new level of consciousness and then begin to explore our inner world, from which our outer world arises.

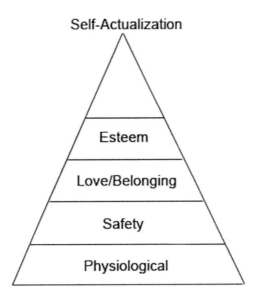

As we climb Maslow's pyramid, we also spiral in consciousness as we look for understanding and purpose in our lives. When we ask the question, "What is my life purpose?" then life begins to take on new meaning.

As we journey on, we come to realize that our outer world is only a reflection of our inner world, and as we become aware of this reality and take responsibility for the insanity we have created for ourselves, we awaken. As we awaken, we are then free to choose another way to walk in the world. We search for a path, "To be in the world, but not of the world," so to speak. We are now in search of that which we truly are, but have forgotten, as we have become mesmerized by the appearance of the outside world and the collective human consciousness. We can now become aware of another aspect of ourselves—that of our higher Self, our Soul.

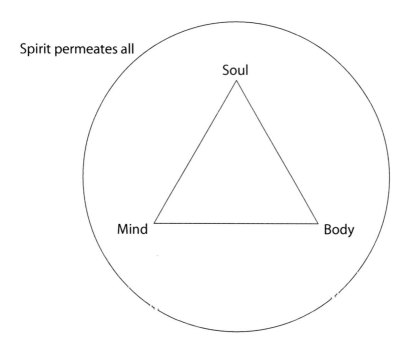

Spirit permeates all

Soul

Mind

Body

The way to the doorway of the Soul is straight and narrow, and it takes focus, determination, and commitment to achieve the evolution of consciousness. For the most part, our journey has now become an inner one; however, we still wax and wane in our ability to stand firm in our knowing of Self. "The Path to Knowing" that I have identified can help us move through the doorway to Self, but we must pass through the eye of the needle in receptive silence to truly experience our Soul consciousness (sometimes called Christ consciousness).

Our experiential awareness of Soul is a choice of "Being," and as we grow and evolve through states and stages of this level of consciousness, we become more expansive and a greater expression of Source.

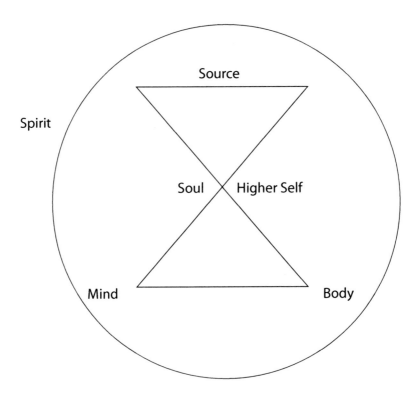

Because our evolution in consciousness is not a straightforward occurrence, we can experience several levels of consciousness within the same moment or within the same day; it is not an exact science, nor is it always predictable or analytical. Our experience *is what it should be* in any given moment as we claim our higher Self and become One with our Soul.

I believe our ultimate experience is one of Soul having a human experience, rather than a human having a spiritual experience. We are creator and co-creator at different states and stages of consciousness, and as we evolve, there is absolutely no separation, for All has become One, as the expression of true love of Oneness. As we continue to evolve, Source and Soul collapse into Oneness, and we are better than home, for we are One with All That Is or has ever been.

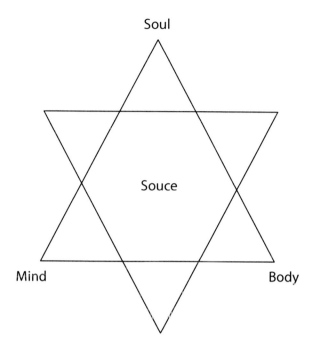

We are our creator, as our creator is us. We co-create and create in unison. The star symbolizes the emergence of what has been called heaven (the fourth dimension) on earth (the third dimension), locked in an experience of Oneness.

The Soulful Living Agreement

I, _____, am committed
to reclaiming my greater Self, that which I Am. I allow myself the
joyful expression of being creator and co-creator in my earthly
experience. I choose to live my potentiality as Soul having a human
experience- -I choose to live Soulfully!

Witness: _____

References

1. Zen Buddhist Stories. Maybe (Taoist story). http://www. katinkahesselink.net/tibet/zen.html. Accessed May 3, 2010.

2. Brainy Quote. Albert Einstein Quotes. http://www.brainyquote. com/quotes/authors/a/albert_einstein_5.html. Accessed May 3, 2010.

3. *American Heritage Dictionary.* 3rd ed. New York, NY: Dell Publishing; 1994.

4. All-Creatures.org. Ralph Waldo Emerson Quotations Archive. http://all-creatures.org/quotes/emerson_ralphwaldo.html. Accessed May 3, 2010.

5. Wikipedia. Maslow's Triangle. http://en.wikipedia.org/wiki/ Maslow's_hierarchy_of_needs. Accessed May 3, 2010.

6. Matthew 16: 24-26. *Holy Bible: A Reader's Guide to Exploring the Holy Bible—King James Version.* Nashville, TN: Thomas Nelson, Inc; 1972.

7. Mark 3: 24-25. *Holy Bible: A Reader's Guide to Exploring the Holy Bible—King James Version.* Nashville, TN: Thomas Nelson, Inc; 1972.

8. Matthew 20: 17-19. *Holy Bible: A Reader's Guide to Exploring the Holy Bible—King James Version.* Nashville, TN: Thomas Nelson, Inc; 1972.

9. Wikipedia. The Wizard of Oz (1939 Film). http://en.wikipedia.org/ wiki/The_Wizard_of_Oz_(1939_film). Accessed May 3, 2010.

About the Author

Cindy Santee is a devoted wife, mother, and registered nurse. She received her Bachelor of Science in Nursing from the University of Illinois at the Medical Center in Chicago. Over her many years of practice, she specialized in oncology and hospice nursing, which she has always found very fulfilling. As she has grown personally and professionally, she has realized that there is more to life than that which appears before us in our everyday existence. She believes that our true purpose in life, individually and collectively, is to evolve and expand in consciousness while having our earthly experience. Through the written word, she invites you to walk through your own doorway of consciousness to become One with your Soul.

The cover of the book is a symbolic representation of Cindy standing in her own Doorway to Knowing. The photos were taken while swimming with the wild dolphins of the Atlantic Ocean, off the coast of the Azores Islands.

CPSIA information can be obtained at www.ICGtesting.com
Printed in the USA
LVOW060707170312

273337LV00003B/6/P

9 781452 076720